Art Across the Alphabet

Art Across the Alphabet

Over **100** Art Experiences That **Enrich Early Literacy**

Kelly Justus Campbell

Illustrated by Kathy Dobbs

Gryphon House
Lewisville, NC

Dedication

I dedicate this book to my family—to my husband for his love and support, to my children, Colin and Mackenzie for their inspiration and laughter, and to my parents for a lifetime of unconditional love and encouragement.

While doing an activity with my preschool-age son, my mother asked if she could make one, too. After a few minutes of watching my mother fill the table with pages of her creations, my son said, "Mommy, I think Grammy needs her own paper." And with that, I also dedicate this book to Grammies and Poppies everywhere because they "need their own paper" too.

Copyright
©2003 Kelly Justus Campbell
Published by Gryphon House, Inc.
PO Box 10, Lewisville, NC 27023
800.638.0928 (toll free); 877.638.7576 (fax)

Visit us on the web at www.gryphonhouse.com

Illustrated by Kathy Dobbs

Reprinted December 2012

Library of Congress Cataloging-in-Publication Data

Campbell, Kelly Justus, 1967
   Art across the alphabet: over 100 art experiences that enrich early literacy / Kelly Justus Campbell; illustrations, Kathy Dobbs.
      p. cm.
   Includes index.
   ISBN13: 978-0-87659-289-2
   1. Art—Study and teaching (Early childhood) Early-childhood education-Activity programs. 3. English language—Alphabet—Study and teaching (Early childhood) I, Title.
LB1139.5.A78C36 2003
372.5—dc21   2002151252

Bulk purchase

Gryphon House books are available for special premiums and sales promotions as well as for fund-raising use. Special editions or book excerpts also can be created to specification. For details, contact the Director of Marketing.

Disclaimer

Table of Contents

Introduction

Art Across the Alphabet is full of fun, art-centered activities to teach children the letters of the alphabet. These original and simple art and craft ideas are designed to reinforce alphabet recognition, develop phonemic awareness and pre-reading skills, and associate reading with fun, while supplementing the letter of the week discovery. Introduce the letters alphabetically, or focus on a letter that corresponds to your curriculum needs.

Letter of the Week

reate the Letter Helper's Hat described below and wear it as the children arrive. During Circle Time, introduce the new letter of the week and pick a helper to wear the hat. Over the course of the entire year, be sure that each child gets at least one turn to wear the hat. Seeing the letter in an unusual way (on your head or a child's head) will provide another opportunity for the children to learn letter recognition. Set aside time during Circle Time to discover the letter of the week. As your helper proudly wears the hat, ask the children if anyone recognizes the letter that the child is wearing.

Letter Helper's Hat

Materials

yarn

ruler

masking tape

corrugated cardboard cut into 2" strips

patterned contact paper, colored construction paper and stickers, or tempera paint

self-sticking Velcro tabs

pencil

colorful tagboard, 12" x 12" squares

adult scissors

utility knife (adult only)

The Creative Process

Measure your head with a piece of yarn. Use masking tape to tape together enough cardboard strips to make a headband that will fit onto your head. Cover the entire headband using the patterned contact paper, construction paper, or tempera paint for a colorful look. Adhere two of the Velcro tabs to the ends of the headband and several along the inside strip so that you can adjust the hat to fit the children and yourself. Next, draw large block letters (one of each letter of the alphabet) onto the tagboard squares and cut them out using scissors, and when necessary, the utility knife. Place the Velcro tabs onto the back of the letter near the bottom. As you discuss each letter, place the appropriate letter onto the headband.

Art Across the Alphabet will provide the children with many unique opportunities to see and hear each letter of the alphabet. This repetition will help reinforce recognition of each letter. Each letter has the following three components—the *Alphabet Gallery Activity*, the *Letter Activities*, and *The Bridge Home*.

Alphabet Gallery

he Alphabet Gallery Activity can be done as the children arrive at school or all together after Circle Time. As the children discover each letter of the alphabet, create an Alphabet Gallery using the process described below. As each letter is completed, hang it on the wall, side by side with the other letters, to create your own Alphabet Gallery around the classroom. Be sure to keep the Alphabet Gallery at the children's eye level. Every time you add a new letter to the Gallery, start at the beginning of the alphabet and point to each letter, asking the children to tell you the letters. When you have completed the entire alphabet, take photos of it with the children underneath. You may have to photograph the gallery in several sections and piece them together after they have been developed. Send the photos or color copies of the photographs home with the children explaining how they created the Alphabet Gallery over the course of the year.

Alphabet Gallery Activity

Materials

roll paper
scissors
fat, black marker
tacky glue

The Creative Process

Cut a 2' x 3' sheet from the roll paper. Use a fat, black marker to draw the letter in large block form, filling the entire sheet. Throughout the book, under the heading "Alphabet Gallery," are suggestions of how to fill in the Alphabet Gallery letter. If there is a child whose name begins with the letter the children are learning, take a picture of that child and ask him or her to hang it on the Alphabet Gallery letter.

Letter Activities

 efore beginning each Letter Activity, write the title of the activity on a piece of sentence strip paper and hang it on the wall or in the Art Center. Before starting the activity, point to the letter the children are learning and say the letter. Each time you pair seeing the letter with saying the letter, you provide another opportunity for recognition of each letter. Ask the designated Letter Helper to stand up. Then, ask the children to remind you what letter you are working on. Explain that the title of the activity starts with the letter of the week. For example, say, "A is for Apple. Apple begins with the letter A." (Point to the letter as you say it, and hold up a piece of tagboard with the letter "A" drawn on it.) "Today, we are going to make apple prints onto a letter A." Explain and demonstrate how to do the activity. As the children work, ask them to tell you what letter they are working on. After the children have completed their projects, hold up one of the creations and ask the children again to identify the letter.

The Bridge Home

section titled "The Bridge Home" follows the letter activities. In this section, you will find reproducible letters to send home to parents to keep them involved in what is happening in your classroom. This section is designed to help build strong parent-teacher relationships. The more parents are involved and kept informed about what is happening in the classroom, the more success you will have with the children. Parents also have a wealth of knowledge and talents that could be beneficial to your curriculum planning. Including families whenever possible will help strengthen family bonds, as well as increase your understanding of each child in your class. For each letter of the alphabet, send a note home explaining what the children learned. Explain that when you provide different opportunities for the children to both see and hear the letters, it increases their ability to recognize the letters. Describe the activities for each letter in your note to the parents, explaining that the art and craft activities provide a fun way to reinforce recognition of the letter that you are working on. Some of the letters have additional activities to include parent and family participation.

Letter Activities

Apple Prints

Materials

roll paper

scissors

fat, black marker

felt

thick cardboard

glue

clothespins, optional

tempera paint

Styrofoam trays or paper plates

paintbrushes

tacky glue

The Creative Process

- Cut a 2' x 3' sheet from the roll paper. Using a fat, black marker, draw the letter "A" in large block form, filling the entire sheet.
- Cut the felt into apple shapes of various sizes.
- Glue the apple shapes onto thick cardboard. The cardboard creates a sturdy backing for printing. You may also wish to glue a clothespin to the back of each "apple stamp" in an upright position for the children to hold onto as they print. Allow the glue to dry.
- Pour a small amount of paint into Styrofoam trays or onto plates.
- Show the children how to dip the apple shapes into the paint or paint it with a paintbrush. Then, press the apple onto the paper.
- Encourage the children to make apple prints on the large letter "A".
- Designate an area of the room to be the Alphabet Gallery. Hang the letter on the wall using tacky glue.

Art Across the Alphabet

A Is for Apple (Print-Making)

Materials
felt

scissors

thick cardboard

glue

tempera paint

Styrofoam trays or paper plates

paintbrushes

colored construction paper

The Creative Process
- Cut the felt into apple shapes, such as whole apple slices (length-wise and width-wise) and apple wedges.
- Glue each apple shape onto a piece of thick cardboard. Allow the glue to dry.
- Pour a small amount of paint into trays or onto plates.
- Encourage the children to dip the felt apple shapes into the paint, or paint them with a paintbrush.
- The children press the apple shapes onto the construction paper.
- Encourage the children to print the apple several times before reapplying paint. The prints with less paint sometimes create a unique effect.
- The children can make apple prints in a variety of colors on the same piece of paper for a rainbow effect.

Hint
Glue the felt apple shapes onto a block of wood to create an apple stamp.

Variation
- Cut out a large letter "A" for each child using colored construction paper. Make sure that each letter "A" is the same size as the construction paper. Encourage the children to print the apple stamps onto the letter "A" using the above technique.

An Army of Ants

Materials

thick cardboard
scissors
red checked tablecloth
masking tape
inkpads
fine-tip markers

The Creative Process

- Cut the cardboard into 8" x 8" squares, one for each child.
- Cut out pieces of the tablecloth to cover one side of each cardboard square. Tape each piece to a cardboard square with the masking tape.
- Draw a block-style letter "A" on each tablecloth-covered square.
- Demonstrate how to create ants by pressing your finger into the inkpad, and then pressing it onto the tablecloth. Place two prints beside each other, touching. Add legs and antennae with the marker.
- Encourage the children to place ants all over their tablecloth.

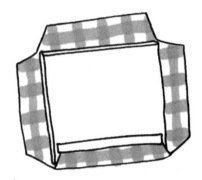

tape to back of cardboard

Airplane Wings

Materials

poster board
scissors
hole punch
tempera paint
paintbrushes
yarn

The Creative Process

- Cut out elongated ovals from the poster board, two for each child.
- Using the hole punch, punch two holes in the top and bottom of each side of the wings. Encourage the children to paint the wings as desired. Allow them to dry.
- Cut strips of yarn. Thread the yarn through the holes in the wings and tie them onto the children's arms.
- The children can fly around the room together to music.

The Bridge Home

Send home the following letter after completing the activities, revising it as necessary.

Dear Parents,

This week, your children learned about the letter "A". Whenever the children see the letter "A" in print and hear it spoken, it reinforces their recognition of the letter. To further reinforce this recognition, we did a number of art activities with titles that begin with the letter "A" or that develop a concept that begins with the letter "A".

Every week, as an introduction to the new letter, the children do some sort of art activity beginning with that letter on a large outline of the particular letter. This is called the "Alphabet Gallery Activity." I have devoted an entire area in our classroom as the Alphabet Gallery. When the children finish decorating the large letter each week, I add it to the "Gallery" by hanging it on the wall.

This past week, the children made "apple prints" all over a large letter "A" for their Alphabet Gallery activity. I cut out apple shapes from felt and glued them onto cardboard. Each child dipped an apple shape into paint, and then pressed it onto the large letter to make a print. I explained that the word "apple" begins with the letter "A". The children also saw the large letter as they made prints, further reinforcing their recognition of it.

The children did various art activities that all began with the letter "A". One activity ("A is for Apple") was an extension of the Alphabet Gallery activity. The children made their own apple prints all over their own pieces of paper. They also created a project called "An Army of Ants." Before they started, I explained what an army of ants was, stressing that "army" and "ant" both begin with the letter "A". I then gave each child a tablecloth-covered square with the letter "A" written on it. The children then made ant prints using their fingers on the square. Finally, the children made "Airplane Wings." We talked about airplanes and how the word starts with the letter "A". The children then decorated their precut wings. After the wings were dry, the children put them on and "flew" around the room while listening to music.

All of these art activities focused on different things that begin with the letter "A" (apples, ants, and airplane wings). This reinforced the children's recognition of the letter "A" because we discussed what the words meant, they saw the letter in print, and they heard it spoken. You can help further the children's recognition of the letter at home by talking about their activities and asking them what they learned.

Sincerely,

Your child's teacher

Button and Band-Aid Collage (Large)

Materials

roll paper
scissors
fat, black marker
buttons and Band-Aids
glue or paste
tacky glue

The Creative Process

- Cut a 2' x 3' sheet from the roll paper. Using a fat, black marker, draw the letter "B" in large block form, filling the entire sheet.
- Help the children glue or paste buttons and/or Band-Aids onto the large letter "B".
- Allow the glue to dry and add this letter to the Alphabet Gallery.

Button and Band-Aid Collage (Small)

Materials

ruler

poster board

pencil

Exacto knife (adult only)

glue or paste

various sizes and shapes of buttons and Band-Aids

The Creative Process

- Measure a 9" x 6" rectangle on the poster board.
- Draw a letter "B", touching all sides of the rectangle.
- Cut out the letter using an Exacto knife (adult only). Be sure to cut out the inside sections of the letter "B" also.
- Repeat this process to make one for each child.
- Demonstrate how to glue or paste the buttons and/or Band-Aids onto the letter.
- Encourage children's creativity. Some children may select certain types of buttons for their collage; some may have overlapping buttons. Let each Button Collage remain unique.
- When the collages are complete, set them aside to dry.

Painting with Letter "B" Paints

Materials

easels
heavy paper
brown, black, and blue tempera paints
paintbrushes

The Creative Process

- Set up each easel with a sheet of heavy paper and the three colors of tempera paint.
- Place a brush into each container of paint, designating a brush for brown, one for black, and one for blue.
- Explain to the children that they are going to paint using color paints that start with the letter "B".
- Before they see the paint, ask the children to guess what the colors might be.
- Encourage the children to create paintings using the three colors. Write each child's name on his painting.

Bubble Prints

Materials

liquid dishwashing soap

water

square pan (approximately 8" x 8")

tempera paints in a variety
   of colors

drinking straw

scissors

white paper

The Creative Process

● Mix equal amounts of water and dishwashing liquid in
the square pan.

● Add tempera paint to the mixture.

● Cut a tiny hole into each straw to prevent the
children from drinking the mixture. Give each child
a straw.

● Encourage the children to take turns blowing into the paint
mixture to fill the pan with bubbles.

● Show the children how to gently touch the paper to the bubbles,
creating a bubble print.

Cut a
tiny hole →

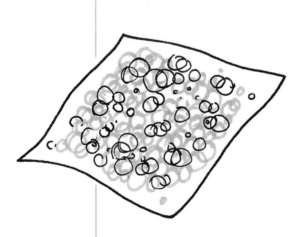

Building Sculptures

Materials
wooden blocks
cardboard blocks
cereal and various grocery boxes
cylindrical oatmeal containers
egg cartons
rectangle sponges

The Creative Process

- Set up a Block Center with a large letter "B" visible.
- Provide the children an opportunity to build using a variety of materials listed above.
- Photograph the children beside their architecture creations when they are complete.
- Create an eye-catching bulletin board display with the photos. (Don't forget to send home the photographs when you take down the bulletin board.)

The Bridge Home

Send home the following letter after completing the activities, revising it as necessary.

Dear Parents,

This week, your children learned about the letter "B". Whenever the children see the letter "B" in print and hear it spoken, their recognition of the letter is reinforced. To further reinforce their recognition of the letter "B", we did a number of art activities with titles that begin with the letter "B" or that develop a concept that begins with the letter "B".

Every week, as an introduction to the new letter, the children do some sort of art activity beginning with that letter on a large outline of the particular letter. This is called the "Alphabet Gallery Activity." I have devoted an entire area in our classroom as the Alphabet Gallery. When the children finish decorating the large letter each week, I add it to the "Gallery" by hanging it on the wall.

This past week, the children glued buttons and Band-Aids all over a large letter "B" for their Alphabet Gallery activity. I explained that the words "button" and "Band-Aids" begin with the letter "B". The children also saw the large letter as they made their collages, further reinforcing their recognition of it.

The children did various art activities that all began with the letter "B". One activity, a smaller version of the "Button and Band-aid Collage" was an extension of the Alphabet Gallery activity. Each child glued buttons and Band-Aids on the letter "B". They also painted designs using "letter B" paints (blue, black, and brown). I explained that brown, black, and blue all begin with the letter "B". The children also made "Bubble Prints". I mixed paint into bubble solution and the children used straws to blow the bubbles. Then they touched paper to the bubbles to make prints. Finally, the children built sculptures using various boxes and blocks. I explained that "blocks" and "build" both begin with the letter "B".

All of these art activities focused on different things that begin with the letter "B" (buttons, Band-Aids, colors that begin with "B", bubbles, blocks, and building). This reinforced the children's recognition of the letter "B" because we discussed what the words meant, they saw the letter in print, and they heard it spoken. You can help further the children's recognition of the letter at home by talking about their activities and asking them what they learned.

Sincerely,

Your child's teacher

Crazy Circular C

Materials

roll paper
scissors
fat, black marker
construction paper
pencil
tacky glue

The Creative Process

- Cut a 2' x 3' sheet from the roll paper. Using a fat, black marker, draw the letter "C" in large block form, filling the entire sheet.
- Draw circles on construction paper.
- Help the children cut out pre-drawn circles to the best of their ability.
- Encourage the children to glue their cutout circles onto the large letter "C".
- Hang the letter in the Alphabet Gallery using tacky glue.

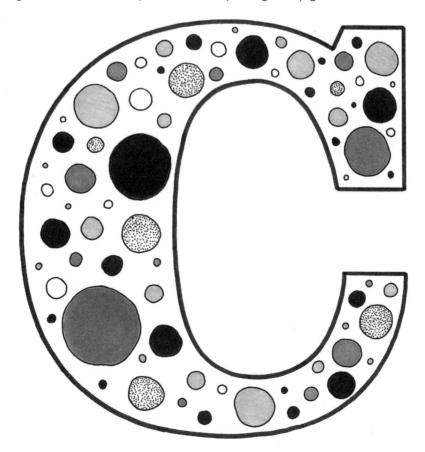

Cutting Collage

Materials

12" x 12" tagboard squares

pencil

scissors

variety of colored and textured papers

glue

The Creative Process

- Draw a letter "C" onto the tagboard, touching all sides of the board. Make one for each child.
- Cut out the letters.
- Ask the children to practice their cutting skills by cutting out pieces from a variety of color and texture papers that will fit onto the cutout letter "C".
- Encourage the children to glue their paper pieces onto the pre-cut letter "C".

Tip

When creating artwork with glue, be sure to explain to the children that paper is very light and does not require much glue to make it stick. Demonstrate how to place a few small dots of glue onto the tagboard to attach a cut-out shape. (You also may want to demonstrate that a blob of glue is too much.)

Car Wheel Creations

Materials

tempera paint

water

paper plates or Styrofoam trays

a variety of toy vehicles with plastic wheels of different sizes

paper

The Creative Process

- Thin the tempera paint with water and pour a small amount onto a plate or tray.
- Encourage the children to "drive" the vehicles through the paint and onto their paper.

Tip

Paint may be difficult to wash off vehicles with wooden wheels, causing a permanent stain.

Creative Cardboard Cars

Materials

large cardboard boxes

utility knife (adult only)

masking tape

large white roll paper

tempera paint, crayons, and markers

colored construction paper

scissors

glue

ruler

ribbon, at least 1½" thick

The Creative Process

● Using the utility knife, cut off the flaps from the top of the box. Then cut off about half of the bottom of the box (adult only).

● Flip the box so that the bottom (with half cut out) is on top.

● Tape down any flaps that stick out. This is the hood of the car.

● If the box has a lot of writing on it, you may want to cover it with white roll paper first.

Remove all flaps on the box top...

flip the box

Cut out a "driver's seat" area

- Encourage the children to use paint, crayons, and markers to decorate the outside of the box. They can also cut out pieces of construction paper and glue them to the box. Older children may wish to add a license plate and lights to make their car more realistic.

- Cut out wheels from paper or cardboard and glue them to the car.

- Cut a slit into the right-hand side of the "hood" of the car, approximately 2" from the open "driver's seat" area (adult only). Repeat this process for the left-hand side of the hood.

- Measure down about 2" on the right-hand side of the back of the car and cut a slit (adult only). Repeat this process for the left-hand side of the back of the car.

- Thread the ribbon through the front right slit and the back right slit and tie it in a knot, creating an arm strap. Repeat this process for the left-hand side.

- Encourage each child to create her own car to take home.

- You may want to ask the children to help you create a few cars to keep in the classroom so they can "drive" throughout the year.

- If you want to help each child create her own car, save enough cardboard boxes until you have one for each child, or ask parents to send in one large box for their child.

The Bridge Home

Send home the following letter after completing the activities, revising it as necessary.

Dear Parents,

This week, your children learned about the letter "C". Whenever the children see the letter "C" in print and hear it spoken, their recognition of the letter is reinforced. To further reinforce their recognition of the letter "C", we did a number of art activities with titles that begin with the letter "C" or that develop a concept that begins with the letter "C".

Every week, as an introduction to the new letter, the children do some sort of art activity beginning with that letter on a large outline of the particular letter. This is called the "Alphabet Gallery Activity." I have devoted an entire area in our classroom as the Alphabet Gallery. When the children finish decorating the large letter each week, I add it to the "Gallery" by hanging it on the wall.

This past week, the children glued circles cut out from construction paper onto a large letter "C" for their Alphabet Gallery activity. I explained that the word "circle" begins with the letter "C". The children also saw the large letter as they glued their circles to it, further reinforcing their recognition of the letter.

The children did various art activities that all began with the letter "C". One activity was a "Cutting Collage." The children cut a variety of papers into pieces and glued them onto a letter "C", creating a collage. I explained that "cutting" and "collage" both begin with the letter "C". They also made "Car Wheel Creations" by "driving" toy cars through paint and then making designs on paper. Finally, the children built cardboard cars. I explained that "cars" begins with the letter "C".

All of these art activities focused on different things that begin with the letter "C" (cutting, collage, and cars). This reinforced the children's recognition of the letter "C" because we discussed what the words meant, they saw the letter in print, and they heard it spoken. You can help further the children's recognition of the letter at home by talking about their activities and asking them what they learned.

Sincerely,

Your child's teacher

Drip, Drop

Materials

roll paper
scissors
fat, black marker
tempera paint in a variety
 of colors
water
paint pans
eyedroppers
tacky glue

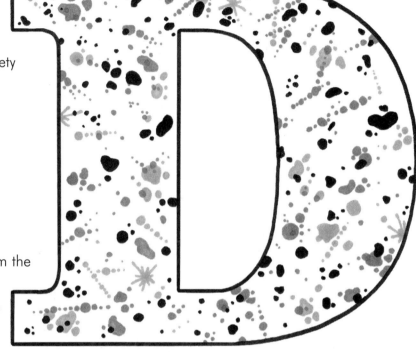

The Creative Process

- Cut a 2' x 3' sheet from the roll paper. Using a fat, black marker, draw the letter "D" in large block form, filling the entire sheet.
- Add water to the tempera paint, watering down the thickness of the paint.
- Pour the thinned paint into shallow pans.
- Demonstrate how to use eyedroppers to suck up paint.
- Encourage the children to drip paint drops from the eyedroppers onto the large letter "D", making sure each child gets a turn. Watch how the colors spread out and mix together.
- Add the letter to the Alphabet Gallery.

D Is for Daddy and Granddaddy

Materials

roll paper

scissors

fat, black marker

photographs of the
children's dads
and granddads

glue

The Creative Process

- Cut a 2' x 3' sheet from the roll paper. Using a fat, black marker, draw the letter "D" in large block form, filling the entire sheet.

- Ask parents to send in pictures of their child's father or grandfather.

- Help the children cut out the faces of their father, grandfather, or special friend.

- Ask the children to glue their pictures to the large letter "D".

- If you have children in your class without fathers and/or grandfathers, ask them to bring in a picture of someone who is like a father or grandfather to them.

Personal Drip Drops

Materials

scissors

felt

permanent markers (adult only)

tempera paint in a variety of colors

water

paint pans

eyedroppers

turkey basters

The Creative Process

- Cut felt into 12" x 12" squares.
- Draw a letter "D" onto the felt squares with the permanent markers, making sure the letter touches all four sides of the felt. Make one felt square for each child.
- Cut out the letters.
- Add water to the tempera paint, watering down the thickness of the paint.
- Pour the thinned paint into shallow pans.
- Encourage the children to use eyedroppers and turkey basters to drip and drop watered-down paint onto the felt letters.

Dragonflies

Materials

tempera paint in a variety of colors

water

paint pans

eyedroppers

coffee filters

clothespins

pipe cleaners

string

The Creative Process

- Add water to tempera paint, watering down the thickness of the paint.
- Pour the thinned paint into shallow paint pans.
- Demonstrate how to use eyedroppers to suck up paint and drip it onto coffee filters, creating a unique design. Watch how the colors spread out and mix together.
- After the coffee filters are dry, gather two filters together in the middle and clip them on a clothespin.
- Add pipe cleaners for antenna and a string for hanging.

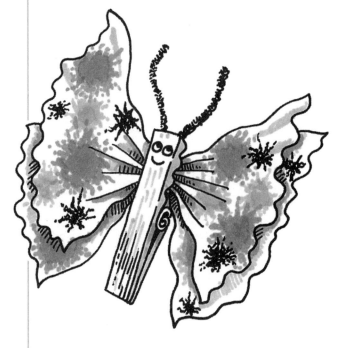

Decorating Doughnuts Extravaganza

Materials

plain doughnuts

icing in tubes, in a variety of colors

scissors

paper plates

marker

clear contact paper

variety of edible sprinkles and jimmies

Polaroid camera

2 buckets and soap, if needed

paper towels

The Creative Process

- Purchase plain doughnuts from your local bakery or supermarket.
- Cut off all the tips from the tubes of icing.
- Write each child's name on a paper plate and cover the name with a small strip of clear contact paper. This will prevent the marker from leaking onto the doughnut or icing.
- Place a doughnut on each plate and pass them out to the children.
- Explain to the children that they are going to decorate their doughnuts in celebration of the letter "D". Tell the children that you will take a picture of their decorated doughnut after they have completed the decoration process, and then they can eat it.

● Encourage the children to decorate their doughnut as creatively as they wish.

● If you do not have a sink in your room, you may wish to have two buckets nearby, one with soap and water, and the other with plain water. Have plenty of paper towels handy.

Fun Bulletin Board

● Take photographs of the doughnut creations, and then make large color photocopies of each creation. Place the enlarged photocopies side by side on the bulletin board with the heading: "Decorating Doughnuts Extravaganza!" Be sure to label each child's name on his doughnut photocopy. Send the original photographs home.

Dog Days

Materials

local animal shelter

The Creative Process

- Invite a representative from a local animal shelter to visit your classroom with puppies. Most animal shelters only charge a small fee to visit your classroom with puppies or kittens.

  Caution: Check for any allergies before scheduling this activity. Also, some children are afraid of dogs.

- Some shelters also will give an educational presentation to your group.

- Ask the representative what kind of an animal he or she plans to bring, or request the person to bring puppies to accompany your letter "D". Some may bring puppies from the shelter that they are trying to find a home for, while others will bring their own adult dogs.

- Make sure to ask if the pet is good with young children.

- Prepare the children before the special four-legged visitors arrive, reminding them to use good manners while the visitors are present.

The Bridge Home

Send home the following letter after completing the activities, revising it as necessary.

Dear Parents,

This week, your children learned about the letter "D". Whenever the children see the letter "D" in print and hear it spoken, their recognition of the letter is reinforced. To further reinforce their recognition of the letter "D", we did a number of art activities with titles that begin with the letter "D" or that develop a concept that begins with the letter "D".

Every week, as an introduction to the new letter, the children do some sort of art activity beginning with that letter on a large outline of the particular letter. This is called the "Alphabet Gallery Activity." I have devoted an entire area in our classroom as the Alphabet Gallery. When the children finish decorating the large letter each week, I add it to the "Gallery" by hanging it on the wall.

This past week, the children used eyedroppers to make "drip drop" designs onto a large letter "D" for their Alphabet Gallery activity. I explained that the words "drip" and "drop" both begin with the letter "D". The children also saw the large letter as they made their designs, further reinforcing their recognition of the letter.

The children made various art projects that all began with the letter "D". One activity was an extension of the Alphabet Gallery. The children made personal drip drop designs on their own small letter "D". The children made dragonflies using coffee filters, paint, and clothespins. I explained that "dragonfly" begins with the letter "D". They decorated doughnuts and ate them for snack. Finally, a visitor from the local animal shelter came in brought some puppies and dogs into the classroom.

All of these activities focused on different things that begin with the letter "D" (drip, drop, dragonfly, doughnut, and dog). This reinforced the children's recognition of the letter "D" because we discussed what the words meant, they saw the letter in print, and they heard it spoken. You can help further the children's recognition of the letter at home by talking about their activities and asking them what they learned.

Sincerely,

Your child's teacher

Note to teacher: If you decide to do the alternate activity, "D Is For Daddy and Granddaddy," change letter accordingly.

Egg-citing Eggs

Materials

roll paper

scissors

fat, black marker

egg-shaped stencils

colored construction paper

crayons, markers, and other
   art materials

tacky glue

The Creative Process

- Cut a 2' x 3' sheet from the roll paper. Using a fat, black marker, draw the letter "E" in large block form, filling the entire sheet.

- Prepare egg-shaped stencils for children to trace around onto colored construction paper. Encourage the children to cut out their egg tracings and decorate these egg shapes with crayons, markers, stickers, or rubber stamps.

- Write each child's name on her egg and glue it to the Alphabet Gallery letter "E".

- Add the letter to the Alphabet Gallery.

Eggshell Mosaics

Materials

eggshells
alcohol (adult only)
paper towels
zipper-closure plastic bags
food coloring
books with pictures of mosaics
tagboard
pencils
white glue

The Creative Process

- Soak the eggshells in alcohol before allowing the children to create with them. After you have soaked them, place them on paper towels to dry. The alcohol will evaporate quickly.
- Crush the shells into smaller pieces by placing them in between two paper towels.
- Place the crushed shells into a few zipper-closure plastic bags. Use one bag for each color that you wish to create.
- Drip a few drops of food coloring into each bag and close the top. Shake the shells around to cover all the pieces completely with food coloring. You may wish to ask the children to help you crush and dye the shells.
- As the eggshell pieces dry, show the children various examples of mosaics for inspiration. The local library is a good source for books with pictures of mosaics.
- Give each child a piece of tagboard.
- Encourage the children to draw a picture, filling the page, without a lot of small, detailed designs. Larger areas to fill in are easier for little hands.
- When the shells are dry, demonstrate how to apply glue to the area of the picture you wish to fill in and then press the mosaic fragments into place.
- When the entire picture has been filled in with mosaic eggshell pieces, allow it to dry flat.

Exciting Envelopes

Materials

envelope

tagboard

marker

scissors

a variety of colorful papers such as wrapping paper,
    colored construction paper, and so on

pencils

glue

large stickers

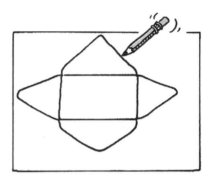

The Creative Process

- Unfold an envelope, being careful not to tear it as you pull open the edges that have glue on them.
- Make several envelope templates by tracing the opened envelope onto tagboard.
- Cut out the templates.
- Encourage the children to trace around the envelope template onto various papers. Help them cut out the envelopes and fold all four tabs in towards the middle of the envelope.
- Place a small amount of glue along the edges of the bottom three tabs and fold them down. (Do not glue the top flap down until the children have placed their letter inside.)
- Allow the envelope to dry before attempting to place mail inside.
- After the envelopes are dry, ask the children to place a note or picture inside the envelope.
- Fold down the top tab. Place a sticker on the tab to hold the envelope closed. (Or, you can place a small amount of glue along the edge of the last tab; however, it will make the envelope harder to open.)

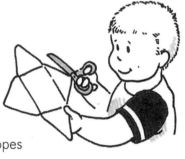

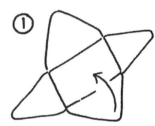

①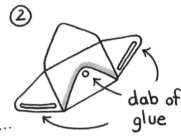

②

fold in...

dab of glue

Variation

● Using large paper and paints, ask the children to create a painting that fills the page. After the painting dries, encourage the children to trace and cut out envelopes following the same process as above. The children can use another section of the painting to create a card and mail it home in the matching envelope! These make great one-of-a-kind birthday cards, thank-you notes, get-well cards, or any-day cards!

Electric Eels

Materials

self-hardening or oven-hardening clay

tempera paint

paintbrushes

The Creative Process

- Give each child a small ball of clay and demonstrate how to roll the ball back and forth on the table until the clay forms a worm-like shape. Explain that this is an eel.

- Encourage the children to decorate their eel by adding pieces of clay to it, curving it into an interesting shape, or leaving it straight.

- If using self-hardening clay, allow it to harden. If using oven-hardening clay, bake it according to the directions (adult only).

- Encourage the children to paint their eels with the tempera paints. Allow them to dry.

The Bridge Home

Send home the following letter after completing the activities, revising it as necessary.

Dear Parents,

This week, your children learned about the letter "E". Whenever the children see the letter "E" in print and hear it spoken, their recognition of the letter is reinforced. To further reinforce their recognition of the letter "E", we did a number of art activities with titles that begin with the letter "E" or that develop a concept that begins with the letter "E".

Every week, as an introduction to the new letter, the children do some sort of art activity beginning with that letter on a large outline of the particular letter. This is called the "Alphabet Gallery Activity." I have devoted an entire area in our classroom as the Alphabet Gallery. When the children finish decorating the large letter each week, I add it to the "Gallery" by hanging it on the wall.

This past week, the children used egg-shaped stencils to trace, cut out, and decorate an egg. Then they glued their eggs onto a large letter "E" for their Alphabet Gallery activity. I explained that the word "egg" begins with the letter "E". The children also saw the large letter as they glued their eggs to it, further reinforcing their recognition of the letter.

The children did various art activities that all began with the letter "E". One activity was "Eggshell Mosaics." Beforehand, I crushed eggshells and used food coloring to color them. Then we discussed what mosaics are, and I showed the children a few examples. The children then glued the dry eggshells onto tagboard to make their own mosaics. Next, we made "Exciting Envelopes." I made some envelope templates, which the children used to trace onto a variety of papers. Then they cut out the envelopes and glued them together. I explained that "exciting" and "envelope" both begin with the letter "E". Finally, they made "Electric Eels." They rolled clay into eel-like shapes and then decorated them after they were hard.

All of these art activities focused on different things that begin with the letter "E" (egg, eggshell, envelope, and eel). This reinforced the children's recognition of the letter "E" because we discussed what the words meant, they saw the letter in print, and they heard it spoken. You can help further the children's recognition of the letter at home by talking about their activities and asking them what they learned.

Sincerely,

Your child's teacher

Fun Fingerpainting

Materials

roll paper
scissors
fat, black marker
fingerpaint
tacky glue

The Creative Process

- Cut a 2' x 3' sheet from the roll paper. Using a fat, black marker, draw the letter "F" in large block form, filling the entire sheet.
- Encourage the children to fingerpaint this large letter "F".
- Encourage them to try to draw the letter "F" with the fingerpaint.
- Hang the letter on the Alphabet Gallery wall.

Fabulous Fingerpaintings

Materials

fingerpaint
fingerpaint paper
permanent marker
music

The Creative Process

- Use a permanent marker to draw a large letter "F" on each sheet of fingerpaint paper, one for each child.
- Next, encourage the children to create a fingerpainting on a large piece of white fingerpaint paper.
- Play soft music as the children create.
- Pass out a second sheet of fingerpaint paper with the letter "F" on it.
- Ask the children to fingerpaint on the letter "F".

Fat Fancy Fish

Materials

large roll paper

scissors

pencils

tempera paint, in a variety of
   bright colors

paintbrushes

masking tape

yarn

glue

newspaper

stapler

blue and green crepe paper, optional

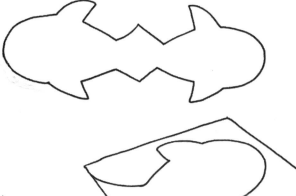

The Creative Process

- Cut off sheets of large roll paper and fold them in half. Give one to each child.

- Help the children draw a large fish on one side of their paper, making sure the fish fills the page. Draw the end of the fish's tail fin so that it touches the fold (see illustration).

- Help the children cut out their fish, making sure to keep the folded part of the paper intact (where the tail meets the fold).

- Encourage the children to paint both sides of their fish using bright, vibrant colors. Allow it to dry.

- Place a 4" strip of masking tape on one side of the fish, either at the top or on the bottom, and only on one half of the fish.

- Tape a strip of yarn to the inside of the top of the fish.

- Explain to the children that they are to place glue around the edges of one of the halves of the fish, but they are to stop gluing when they come to the 4" masking tape strip.

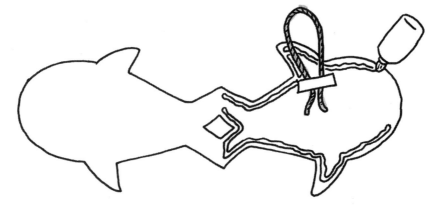

- Next, fold the unglued half of the fish onto the glued half.
- After the glue is dry, stuff the fish with crumpled balls of newspaper and glue or staple the hole closed.
- Hang the fish around the room or in the hallway.
- If desired, hang strips of blue and green crepe paper in between the fish to add to the "underwater" classroom.

Stuff with
crumpled newspaper

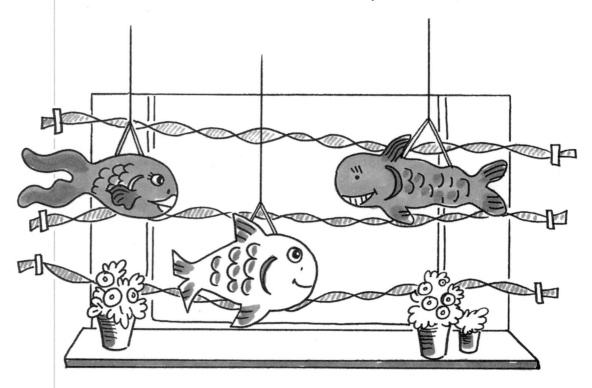

Family Portraits

Materials

pencils

18" x 24" paper

markers, crayons, tempera paint in a variety of colors, and watercolor paints

The Creative Process

- Ask the children to draw a picture of all the family members in their family, including themselves and any pets they have.
- Encourage them to use markers, crayons, and tempera or watercolor paints to add color to the drawings.
- Hang the portraits in the room.

Bulletin Board Activity

Hang each family portrait painting on top of a photograph of the family, covering the entire photograph. Be sure to staple only the top of the family portrait paintings, so that they can be lifted to reveal the photograph underneath. Label each photograph with the appropriate family name. Title the bulletin board "Family Find: Can You Guess Whose Family This Is?"

The Bridge Home

Send home the following letter after completing the activities, revising it as necessary.

Dear Parents,

This week, your children learned about the letter "F". Whenever the children see the letter "F" in print and hear it spoken, their recognition of the letter is reinforced. To further reinforce their recognition of the letter "F", we did a number of art activities with titles that begin with the letter "F" or that develop a concept that begins with the letter "F".

Every week, as an introduction to the new letter, the children do some sort of art activity beginning with that letter on a large outline of the particular letter. This is called the "Alphabet Gallery Activity." I have devoted an entire area in our classroom as the Alphabet Gallery. When the children finish decorating the large letter each week, I add it to the "Gallery" by hanging it on the wall.

This past week, the children fingerpainted on a large letter "F" for their Alphabet Gallery activity. I explained that the word "fingerpaint" begins with the letter "F". The children also saw the large letter as they made their designs, further reinforcing their recognition of the letter.

The children did various art activities that all began with the letter "F". As an extension of the Alphabet Gallery activity, the children fingerpainted on their own paper and letter "F". Another activity was "Fat Fancy Fish." The children drew a large fish shape on a large sheet of paper folded in half. They then cut out the fish, decorated it, and stuffed it with paper. I explained that the "fish" were "fat" and "fancy," all of which start with the letter "F". Finally, the children drew portraits of their families ("family" begins with "F").

All of these art activities focused on different things that begin with the letter "F" (fingerpaint, fish, and family). This reinforced the children's recognition of the letter "F" because we discussed what the words meant, they saw the letter in print, and they heard it spoken. You can help further the children's recognition of the letter at home by talking about their activities and asking them what they learned.

Sincerely,

Your child's teacher

Giant Green G

Materials

roll paper
scissors
fat, black marker
green, white, and black tempera paint
margarine tubs or baby food jars
paintbrushes
tacky glue

The Creative Process

- Cut a 2' x 3' sheet from the roll paper. Using a fat, black marker, draw the letter "G" in large block form, filling the entire sheet.
- Show the children how to mix green tempera paint with white and black to create various shades of green.
- Save the various shades of green paint in margarine tubs or baby food jars.
- Provide small paintbrushes for the children to paint the large letter "G" using the different shades of green.
- Add the letter to the Alphabet Gallery.

Personal Giant Green G's

Materials

tagboard

scissors

permanent marker

Styrofoam egg cartons

green, white, and black tempera paint

paintbrushes

The Creative Process

- Cut tagboard into 12" x 12" squares.
- Using a permanent marker, draw a letter "G" on each tagboard square, filling the entire square. Make one for each child.
- Pass out the egg cartons and encourage the children to experiment with mixing green tempera paint with white or black tempera paint to create lighter and darker green tones in the egg cartons.
- The children decorate their own letter "G" using the various shades of green with small paintbrushes.

Giant Games (Hopscotch)

Materials

primed canvas on a roll or large, white roll paper

scissors

permanent black marker

yardstick

pencils

tempera paint

paintbrushes

Polaroid camera

The Creative Process

- (Make one hopscotch court to be kept in the classroom, or let each child create his own to take home.)

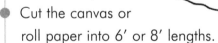

- Cut the canvas or roll paper into 6' or 8' lengths.
- Using a permanent black marker and a yardstick, draw hopscotch lines on the canvas or large roll paper.
- Ask the children to design each block of the hopscotch court using pencils.
- Next, encourage the children to add color to their design using the tempera paint.
- Allow to dry, and then play a game of hopscotch!
- Use a Polaroid camera to take pictures of the children using their creations.

Giant Games (Tic-Tac-Toe)

Materials

primed canvas on a roll or large, white roll paper

scissors

permanent black marker

yardstick

12 squares of tagboard

pencils

markers or tempera paint

paintbrushes

The Creative Process

- (Create one Tic-Tac-Toe board to keep in your classroom, or allow each child to create one to take home.)
- Cut out a large square from the canvas or large roll paper.
- Draw the Tic-Tac-Toe grid lines on the large square using a black permanent marker and a yardstick.
- Encourage the children to decorate the tagboard squares using pencils, markers, and paint. Ask them to create two different decorations on two different tagboard squares. These will be the playing pieces for the two different players.
- Ask the children to create six tagboard squares for each pattern.
- Allow to dry and play!

LETTER G ACTIVITIES

Giant Games (Puzzles)

Materials

12" x 12" tagboard squares
markers
pencils
scissors

The Creative Process

- Give each child a tagboard square. Help the children create a picture on the tagboard with at least one letter "G" hidden in the composition.
- Ask the children to turn the pictures over and help them to draw puzzle pieces on the back.
- Help the children cut out the puzzle pieces.
- The children can turn over the pieces and try to put the puzzle back together again.
- Ask the children to exchange puzzles and try to put them back together again.
- Remind the children to look for the hidden letter "G"!

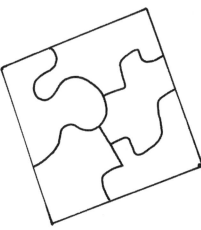

The Bridge Home

Send home the following letter after completing the activities, revising it as necessary.

Dear Parents,

This week, your children learned about the letter "G". Whenever the children see the letter "G" in print and hear it spoken, it reinforces their recognition of the letter. To further reinforce this recognition, we did a number of art activities with titles that begin with the letter "G" or that develop a concept that begins with the letter "G".

Every week, as an introduction to the new letter, the children do some sort of art activity beginning with that letter on a large outline of the particular letter. This is called the "Alphabet Gallery Activity." I have devoted an entire area in our classroom as the Alphabet Gallery. When the children finish decorating the large letter each week, I add it to the "Gallery" by hanging it on the wall.

This past week, the children painted designs on a large letter "G" using various shades of green for their Alphabet Gallery activity. The children experimented with mixing green, white, and black tempera paint to make different shades of green. I explained that the word "green" begins with the letter "G". The children also saw the large letter as they made their designs, further reinforcing their recognition of the letter.

The children did various art activities that all began with the letter "G". As an extension of the Alphabet Gallery activity, the children made their own "Green G's" by mixing green, white, and black tempera paint to make various shades of green paint. We also made "Giant Games"—Hopscotch, Tic-Tac-Toe, and Puzzles. The children designed blocks for a giant hopscotch court, they helped design a giant Tic-Tac-Toe board, and they made puzzle boards. I explained that "giant" and "game" both begin with the letter "G".

All of these art activities focused on different things that begin with the letter "G" (green, giant, and game). This reinforced the children's recognition of the letter "G" because we discussed what the words meant, they saw the letter in print, and they heard it spoken. You can help further the children's recognition of the letter at home by talking about their activities and asking them what they learned.

Sincerely,

Your child's teacher

Happy Handprints

Materials

roll paper

fat, black marker

paper towels

pie tin

tempera paint

tacky glue

The Creative Process

- Cut a 2' x 3' sheet from the roll paper. Using a fat, black marker, draw the letter "H" in large block form, filling the entire sheet.
- Fold paper towels to fit into the pie tin.
- Pour paint on top of the paper towels.
- Encourage each child to place her hand onto the paint-covered paper towel, and then put her handprint onto the letter "H".
- Label each handprint with the child's name.
- Add the letter to the Alphabet Gallery.

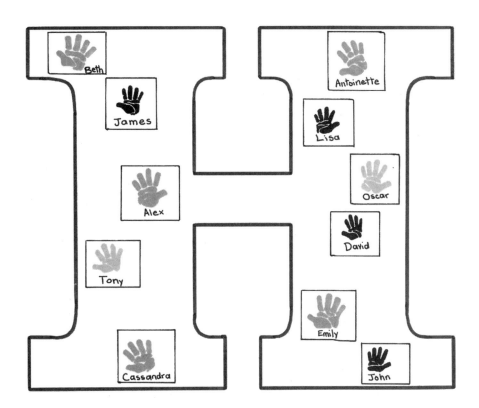

Hurray for Hats!

This is a good activity to ask for parent volunteers to come in and help!
(Create a hat and attach a new letter using self-stick Velcro and wear it on the
day that you introduce a new letter. Ask the Helper of the Day to wear it.)

Materials

string

thick cardboard

scissors

markers

stapler or masking tape

balloons

flour

water

bucket

newspaper strips

paint

paintbrushes

colored construction paper, tissue paper, and fabric

The Creative Process

- Measure the circumference of each child's head with a
  string. (Add an inch to allow for shrinking.)
- Cut thick cardboard into 2" strips.
- Cut a cardboard strip to the
  size of each string, allowing an
  extra 1½" for overlap.
- Label the inside of the
  headband with each child's name.
- Staple or tape the cardboard strip into a circle.

TIM ← 1½" →

TIM

← staple!

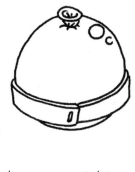

- Blow up a balloon to fit inside of the cardboard strip headband and place it inside the headband.
- In the bucket, mix flour and water to make papier-mâché. (The consistency should be like a wet paste.)
- Put the newspaper strips into the paste mixture and cover them completely with the paste.
- Show the children how to place two layers of the newspaper strips all over the balloon, covering the entire balloon and cardboard areas. Allow to dry.
- Now is the fun part. Encourage the children to paint their hats.
- After the paint dries, pop the balloon and pull it out. **CAUTION**: This step should be done by adults only!
- Next, the children can add fabric, tissue paper, and construction paper for the details. Encourage the children to be creative!
- After the hats are dry, have a hat parade!

Cover completely and let dry!

Happy Hermit Crabs

Materials

tagboard

scissors

A House for Hermit Crab by Eric Carle

glue

tissue paper in a variety of colors

The Creative Process

● Draw a simple seashell shape onto a piece of tagboard and cut it out. Make one for each child.

● Read *A House for Hermit Crab* to the children.

● Encourage the children to create their own unique hermit crab home by tearing small pieces of tissue paper, rolling them into balls, and gluing the balls onto the tagboard shell. Allow them to dry.

Tip

Another great children's story about a hermit crab is *Is This a House for Hermit Crab?* by Megan McDonald and S.D. Schindler.

LETTER H ACTIVITIES

Home Sweet Home

Materials

small cardboard boxes
colored construction paper
glue
scissors
tempera paint
paintbrushes

The Creative Process

● Discuss different characteristics of a house with the children. For example, they usually have windows and a door; some have chimneys; they may be constructed from bricks, wood, aluminum siding, or logs; some have window boxes filled with flowers; some have shutters; and so on.

● Next, give each child a small cardboard box to make their own miniature house.

● Encourage them to use the construction paper and paint to create the details of their house. Allow them to dry.

The Bridge Home

Send home the following letter after completing the activities, revising it as necessary.

Dear Parents,

This week, your children learned about the letter "H". Whenever the children see the letter "H" in print and hear it spoken, it reinforces their recognition of the letter. To further reinforce their recognition of the letter "H", we did a number of art activities with titles that begin with the letter "H" or that develop a concept that begins with the letter "H".

Every week, as an introduction to the new letter, the children do some sort of art activity beginning with that letter on a large outline of the particular letter. This is called the "Alphabet Gallery Activity." I have devoted an entire area in our classroom as the Alphabet Gallery. When the children finish decorating the large letter each week, I add it to the "Gallery" by hanging it on the wall.

This past week, the children made "happy handprints" on a large letter "H" for their Alphabet Gallery activity. I explained that the words "happy" and "handprint" begin with the letter "H". The children also saw the large letter as they made their handprints, further reinforcing their recognition of the letter.

The children did various art activities that all began with the letter "H". We made papier-mâché hats. I gave each child a cardboard headband with a balloon inside of it. The children dipped newspaper strips into papier-mâché paste and put them all over the balloons. After they were dry, we popped the balloons. The children then decorated their hats and we had a parade! I explained that "hat" begins with the letter "H". Another activity was making hermit crab homes. First, I read them *A House for Hermit Crab* by Eric Carle. Then I gave them tagboard seashells to decorate using balls of tissue paper and glue. I explained that "happy," "hermit," and "house" all begin with the letter "H". In addition, the book reinforced the concept. Finally, the children made their own homes out of cardboard.

All of these art activities focused on different things that begin with the letter "H" (hat, happy, hermit, home, and house). This reinforced the children's recognition of the letter "H" because we discussed what the words meant, they saw the letter in print, and they heard it spoken. You can help further the children's recognition of the letter at home by talking about their activities and asking them what they learned.

Sincerely,

Your child's teacher

Indigo Ice Cube Paintings

Materials

large roll paper

scissors

fat, black marker

indigo-colored tempera paint (Indigo is a shade of blue.)

small paper or plastic cups

water

plastic spoons

freezer

tacky glue

The Creative Process

- Cut a 2' x 3' sheet from the roll paper. Using a fat, black marker, draw the letter "I" in large block form, filling the entire sheet.
- Pour indigo paint into the cups, filling them approximately ¼ full. Then pour water into the same cups and stir the mixture with a plastic spoon. Make one for each child.
- Leave the spoons in the cups for the children to use as a handle for painting when frozen. (The spoon does not need to be standing perfectly upright—it is okay if it rests on the side of the cup and is slanted.)
- Place the filled cups into the freezer until the paint is frozen completely.
- Once frozen, remove the cups from the freezer and twist the "Indigo Ice Cube" from each cup.

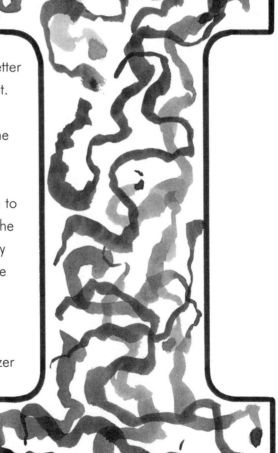

● Ask the children to paint with them on the large letter "I". As the cube melts, it will leave a unique paint trail.

● **Caution**: Be sure to stress to the children that this is NOT a Popsicle—it is frozen paint and is not to be eaten.

● Let it dry. Add the letter to the Alphabet Gallery.

Tip

If you want a more colorful painting, freeze a variety of colors of tempera paint using the same process, and allow the children to paint with these.

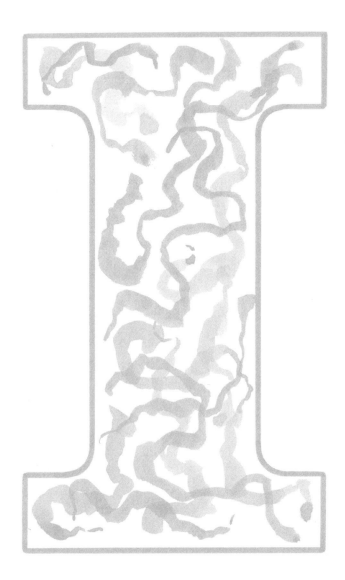

Ideal Ice Cream

Materials

tagboard

scissors

pencils

construction paper in a variety of colors

glue

markers

The Creative Process

- Cut out ice cream cone-shaped stencils about 5" long and circle-shaped stencils about 4" in diameter from tagboard.
- Help the children trace the cone-shaped stencil and cut it out.
- Then help them trace the circle shapes onto various colors of construction paper, creating ice-cream scoops.
- Ask the children to glue the ice-cream scoops to the top of their cone.
- They can use the markers to decorate the scoops with sprinkles and chips. Don't forget to add a cherry on top!
- Share the following fun facts with the children while they are making their cones:

* The ice cream sundae was created to be sold on Sundays ("The Lord's Day"), when slurping an ice cream soda was not permitted. The ice cream sundae was quieter than a soda, and the spelling was changed so as not to appear to be mocking the "Lord's Day."

* The ice cream cone was introduced at the St. Louis Exposition of 1904 when an ice cream vendor ran out of bowls. A neighboring pastry maker rolled thin wafers into cone shapes, called them "cornucopias," and sold them to the ice cream concessionaire to use instead of bowls.

YUM!

Imaginative Inventions

Materials

books about flying machines (see below)
18" x 24" white paper
pencils
colored pencils

The Creative Process

- Borrow books from your local library showing various flying machines. Some good examples are *Christopher's Little Airplane* by Mark S. James, *Minton Goes Flying* by Anna Fienberg, *Flying in a Hot Air Balloon* by Cheryl Walsh Bellville, *Hot Air Balloons* by Ailsa Spindler, *Hot Air Balloons* by Christine Kalakuka, and *Lighter Than Air: An Illustrated History of the Development of Hot-air Balloons and Airships* by David Owen.
- Discuss what makes each machine go up in the air.
- Encourage the children to draw their own flying machine using the paper and pencils.
- The children can add color to their pictures with colored pencils.

Impressive Impressions

Materials

self-hardening clay or clay that must be baked to harden

rolling pins

plastic knives

objects that will create impressions, such as acorns, wheat stalks, various ornamental grasses, leaves, seashells, screws, matchbox cars, blocks with raised letters, rope, shoes, plastic cups to create circle shapes, and so on

drinking straw

tempera paint

paintbrushes

yarn

The Creative Process

- Show the children how to roll the clay flat with a rolling pin, and then cut it into a shape, using a plastic knife.
- Next, encourage the children to press various objects into the clay and lift them back out, creating impressions in the clay.
- Use a drinking straw to poke a hole in the clay near the top for hanging.
- If the clay needs to be baked, place it into the oven and follow the directions on the package for baking (adult only). If the clay is self-hardening, allow it to dry outside in the sun or by a window.
- After the clay impressions are completely dry and hard, paint them with tempera paint. Use a small amount of paint. Using too much paint will completely fill in the impressions, covering them over and making them impossible to see.
- Lace a piece of yarn through the hole for hanging.

The Bridge Home

Send home the following letter after completing the activities, revising it as necessary.

Dear Parents,

This week, your children learned about the letter "I". Whenever the children see the letter "I" in print and hear it spoken, it reinforces their recognition of the letter. This week, we did a number of art activities with titles that begin with the letter "I" or that develop a concept that begins with the letter "I".

Every week, as an introduction to the new letter, the children do some sort of art activity beginning with that letter on a large outline of the particular letter. This is called the "Alphabet Gallery Activity." I have devoted an entire area in our classroom as the Alphabet Gallery. When the children finish decorating the large letter each week, I add it to the "Gallery" by hanging it on the wall.

This past week, the children made designs on a large letter "I" using indigo-colored ice cubes for their Alphabet Gallery activity. I explained that the words "indigo" and "ice" begin with the letter "I". The children also saw the large letter as they made their designs, further reinforcing their recognition of the letter.

The children did various art activities that all began with the letter "I". They made ice cream cones out of tagboard. They also made "imaginative inventions." First, I read them some books about various flying machines. We discussed what "inventions" are. Then the children used their "imaginations" to "invent" and draw their own flying machine. Finally, the children made "impressive impressions" by pressing objects into soft clay and then allowing the clay to harden.

All of these art activities focused on different things that begin with the letter "I" (ice cube, ice cream, imaginative, invention, and impression). This reinforced the children's recognition of the letter "I" because we discussed what the words meant, they saw the letter in print, and they heard it spoken. You can help further the children's recognition of the letter at home by talking about their activities and asking them what they learned.

Sincerely,

Your child's teacher

Jump Prints

Materials

roll paper

fat, black marker

tempera paint in a variety of colors

paintbrush

marker

scissors

tacky glue

The Creative Process

- Cut a 2' x 3' sheet from the roll paper. Using a fat, black marker, draw the letter "J" in large block form, filling the entire sheet.
- Paint the bottom of the children's rubber-soled tennis shoes with various colors of tempera paint. Each child gets a different color of paint.
- Encourage the children to jump on the alphabet letter. If the children jump on top of other footprints, it will create a unique, overlapping design.
- Label their "jump prints" with their names.
- Hang the letter on the Alphabet Gallery wall.

Clean-Up Tips: Before doing this activity, send a note home to parents suggesting that their child wear old shoes for this activity. For easy cleanup, use washable paint and keep a bucket of soapy water nearby.

Personal Jump Prints

Materials

18" x 24" white paper

tempera paint

paintbrush

black marker

The Creative Process

- Before doing the Alphabet Gallery activity and this activity, print a large letter "J" onto pieces of 18" x 24" white paper, one for each child.
- While the children still have paint on their shoes from the Alphabet Gallery activity, ask them to jump on their own letter "J" paper.
- Label the Jump Prints with the child's names.

Jacks-in-a-Box Painting

Materials

tempera paint in a variety of colors

zipper-closure plastic sandwich bags

game of jacks

paper

department store shirt box or shoebox with lid

plastic spoons

The Creative Process

- Squeeze or spoon a few drops of each color of tempera paint into separate plastic bags.
- Place several jacks into each bag with the paint. You can also add the ball for a different effect.
- Shake the bags until the jacks and ball are coated with paint.
- Place one sheet of paper inside the box.
- Designate one plastic spoon for each bag of colored paint. Scoop out the jacks and place them on the paper inside the box.
- Place the lid on the box and shake.
- Open the lid to reveal your creation!

Put on the lid and SHAKE!

Tip

If you have a classroom of children, you will want more than one game of jacks and several boxes to allow several children the opportunity to create at the same time.

Jar Prints

Materials

tempera paint

paint trays

18" x 24" paper

jars in a variety of shapes and sizes

The Creative Process

- Pour a variety of colors of tempera paint into paint trays.
- Give each child a sheet of 18" x 24" paper.
- Demonstrate how to dip the rims and bottoms of the jars into the paint trays and print them onto the paper. For those jars with raised printing on the sides, try printing the side of the jar.
- Encourage the children to repeat the above process, creating an interesting pattern all over their paper.

Jeans for J

Materials

tagboard
black marker
scissors
old pair of blue jeans
tacky glue

The Creative Process

- Draw a block-style letter "J" onto a piece of tagboard, filling the entire page. Cut out the letter "J". Make one for each child.
- Cut the blue jeans into a variety of small shapes.
- Ask the children to "dress" their letter "J" in jeans by gluing the pieces of jeans onto their letter.

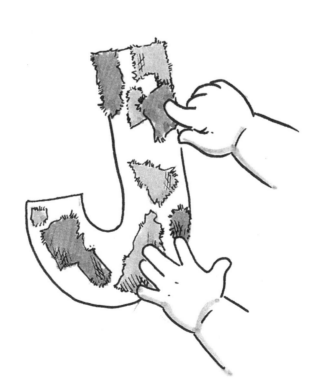

The Bridge Home

Send home the following letter after completing the activities, revising it as necessary.

Dear Parents,

This week, your children learned about the letter "J". Whenever the children see the letter "J" in print and hear it spoken, it reinforces their recognition of the letter. To further reinforce their recognition of the letter "J", we did a number of art activities with titles that begin with the letter "J" or that develop a concept that begins with the letter "J".

Every week, as an introduction to the new letter, the children do some sort of art activity beginning with that letter on a large outline of the particular letter. This is called the "Alphabet Gallery Activity." I have devoted an entire area in our classroom as the Alphabet Gallery. When the children finish decorating the large letter each week, I add it to the "Gallery" by hanging it on the wall.

This past week, the children made jump prints on a large letter "J" for their Alphabet Gallery activity. I painted the bottom of the children's shoes using a paintbrush and the children jumped on top of the letter. I explained that the word "jump" begins with the letter "J". The children also saw the large letter as they jumped, further reinforcing their recognition of the letter.

The children did various art activities that all began with the letter "J". As an extension of the alphabet gallery activity, the children made personal jump prints on their own letter "J". They also made designs using a game of jacks. I put jacks into plastic bags with paint and shook the bags until the jacks were coated. Then, the children put paper into a box, scooped some jacks into the box, put the lid on, and shook them. The jacks made creative designs on each child's paper. The children also made prints using jars. Finally, they made "jean" collages (by gluing denim pieces onto a letter "J").

All of these art activities focused on different things that begin with the letter "J" (jump, jacks, jar, and jeans). This reinforced the children's recognition of the letter "J" because we discussed what the words meant, they saw the letter in print, and they heard it spoken. You can help further the children's recognition of the letter at home by talking about their activities and asking them what they learned.

Sincerely,

Your child's teacher

Kitten Prints

Materials

roll paper

fat, black marker

kitten paw print stamp or shoe insert, scissors, glue, and block

tempera paint or inkpad

Styrofoam tray or paper plate

tacky glue

The Creative Process

- Cut a 2' x 3' sheet from the roll paper. Using a fat, black marker, draw the letter "K" in large block form, filling the entire sheet.
- Purchase a stamp of a kitten paw print or make your own by cutting a shoe insert into the shape of a kitten paw print and then gluing the paw print shape onto a block.
- Pour a thin layer of paint into a tray or plate or use an inkpad.
- Encourage the children to stamp kitten paw prints on the letter "K".
- Add the letter to the Alphabet Gallery.

Kool-Aid and Glue Collage

Materials

12" x 12" tagboard squares

scissors

white glue

Kool-Aid powdered drink mix in a variety of flavors

plastic spoons

The Creative Process

- Cut each tagboard square into a letter "K".
- Create designs by dripping or spreading glue on the tagboard letter "K" cutouts.
- Sprinkle the powdered Kool-Aid over the glue using the plastic spoons.
- Use different flavors of Kool-Aid to create a variety of colors in the designs.
- Shake off the excess powder and allow to dry.

Kooky Kites

Materials

nylon parachute material
scissors
thin dowel rods
clippers (to cut the dowel rods)
fabric paint
paintbrushes
fabric glue
thin string
toilet paper rolls

The Creative Process

- Cut out large, diamond kite shapes from the nylon material.
- Measure the kite shape from the top point to the bottom point and cut a dowel rod to this measurement.
- Measure the kite shape from the point on the left to the point on the right and cut a dowel rod to this measurement.
- Encourage the children to decorate their kites using the fabric paints.
- When dry, glue the dowel rods at the top and bottom points of the kite and glue the other dowel rod at the left and right points of the kite.
- Glue on a tail using scraps of leftover material.
- Wrap plenty of string around the toilet paper roll.
- Place a dowel rod, cut at least 2" longer than the toilet paper roll, inside of the toilet paper roll.
- When the kite is dry, attach one end of the string at the point where the dowel rods cross.
- Take the children outside to fly a kite!

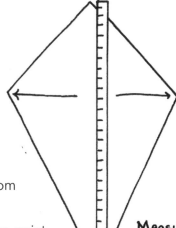

Measure point-to-point and cut dowels to match.

Glue on tail.

Kaleidoscopes

Materials

construction paper
scissors
white drawing paper
glue
thin markers

The Creative Process

- Cut out several 2"-high letter "K"'s from construction paper.
- Give each child a piece of drawing paper. Encourage the children to glue the letters all over their paper, allowing some to touch and overlap.
- Allow them to dry.
- Next, ask the children to fill in some or all of the areas and small spaces between the letters using thin markers. The finished product will resemble a kaleidoscope image.

The Bridge Home

Send home the following letter after completing the activities, revising it as necessary.

Dear Parents,

This week, your children learned about the letter "K". Whenever the children see the letter "K" in print and hear it spoken, it reinforces their recognition of the letter. This week, we did a number of art activities with titles that begin with the letter "K" or that develop a concept that begins with the letter "K".

Every week, as an introduction to the new letter, the children do some sort of art activity beginning with that letter on a large outline of the particular letter. This is called the "Alphabet Gallery Activity." I have devoted an entire area in our classroom as the Alphabet Gallery. When the children finish decorating the large letter each week, I add it to the "Gallery" by hanging it on the wall.

This past week, the children made kitten paw prints on a large letter "K" for their Alphabet Gallery activity. Beforehand, I made paw print stamps. The children dipped the kitten paw prints into paint and made prints all over the "K". I explained that the word "kitten" begins with the letter "K". The children also saw the large letter as they jumped, further reinforcing their recognition of the letter.

The children did various art activities that all began with the letter "K". They made "Kool-Aid and Glue Collages" by spreading glue all over their own tagboard "K" and then sprinkling dry Kool-Aid on top of the glue. They shook off the excess powder and let it dry. I explained that "Kool-Aid" begins with "K" (and they also saw the letter "K"). They made their own kites, and we took them outside and flew them. Finally, they made kaleidoscopes using small cutout letter "K"'s. I explained what kaleidoscopes were before they began.

All of these art activities focused on different things that begin with the letter "K" (kitten, Kool-Aid, kite, and kaleidoscope). This reinforced the children's recognition of the letter "K" because we discussed what the words meant, they saw the letter in print, and they heard it spoken. You can help further the children's recognition of the letter at home by talking about their activities and asking them what they learned.

Sincerely,

Your child's teacher

Leaf Prints

Materials

roll paper

fat, black marker

paint

Styrofoam trays or paper plates

paper towels

leaves

tacky glue

The Creative Process

- Cut a 2' x 3' sheet from the roll paper. Using a fat, black marker, draw the letter "L" in large block form, filling the entire sheet.
- Pour a small amount of paint into a tray or plate.
- Show the children how to dip one side of a leaf into the paint, dab the excess paint onto a paper towel, and then press the leaf onto the letter "L".
- Add the letter to the Alphabet Gallery.

Art Across the Alphabet

Leaf, Lego, and Lace Prints

Materials

tagboard

scissors

leaves

Legos

pieces of lace

knife

paper towels

tempera paint in various colors

The Creative Process

- Cut out a large letter "L" from a piece of tagboard.
- Show the children how to dip one side of a leaf into the paint, dab the excess paint onto a paper towel, and then press the leaf onto the paper.
- Explain that it is possible to print the leaf a few times before adding more paint. This creates a nice effect and in most cases, the less paint on the leaf, the more detail you can see.
- Repeat with the Legos and the lace.

Lively Lines

Materials
tagboard
pipe cleaners
glue

The Creative Process
- Give each child a piece of tagboard and a few pipe cleaners.
- Ask the children to create a "line collage" by gluing the pipe cleaners onto the tagboard. Encourage them to create a unique design by bending the pipe cleaners and overlapping them.
- Allow them to dry.

Variation
- Encourage the children to stick pipe cleaners into a small block of Styrofoam. Encourage them to bend the pipe cleaners and twist them together to create a longer line.

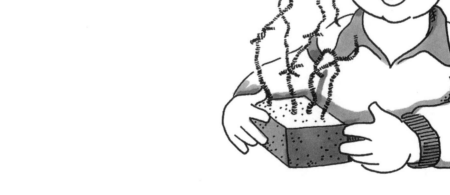

Art Across the Alphabet

Liquid Paintings

Materials

drop cloth

easels

paper

tempera paint

water

smocks

eyedroppers and turkey basters

The Creative Process

- Place a drop cloth on the floor and arrange the easels on top of it.
- Clip a piece of paper onto each easel.
- Add water to the tempera paint so that it is a bit runny.
- Place an eyedropper, a turkey baster, and a smock at each easel.
- Demonstrate how to dip the eyedropper and turkey baster into the watered-down paint, place it at the top of the sheet, and squeeze to release a bit of the paint. Watch as the paint drips down the paper.
- Ask each child to put on a smock.
- Encourage the children to repeat the process. Encourage them to use a variety of colors.

The Bridge Home

Send home the following letter after completing the activities, revising it as necessary.

Dear Parents,

This week, your children learned about the letter "L". Whenever the children see the letter "L" in print and hear it spoken, it reinforces their recognition of the letter. This week, we did a number of art activities with titles that begin with the letter "L" or that develop a concept that begins with the letter "L".

Every week, as an introduction to the new letter, the children do some sort of art activity beginning with that letter on a large outline of the particular letter. This is called the "Alphabet Gallery Activity." I have devoted an entire area in our classroom as the Alphabet Gallery. When the children finish decorating the large letter each week, I add it to the "Gallery" by hanging it on the wall.

This past week, the children made leaf prints on a large letter "L" for their Alphabet Gallery activity. The children dipped leaves into paint and made prints on the paper. I explained that the word "leaf" begins with the letter "L". The children also saw the large letter as they made their prints, further reinforcing their recognition of the letter.

The children did various art activities that all began with the letter "L". As an extension of the alphabet gallery activity, the children made prints using leaves, Legos, and lace. I explained that all three of the items begin with the letter "L". They also made "line collages" by gluing pipe cleaners to tagboard. Finally, they made "liquid paintings" by dipping eyedroppers and turkey basters into watered-down paint and making designs on paper. The paper was on easels, causing the paint to run and look "liquid."

All of these art activities focused on different things that begin with the letter "L" (leaf, Legos, lace, line, and liquid). This reinforced the children's recognition of the letter "L" because we discussed what the words meant, they saw the letter in print, and they heard it spoken. You can help further the children's recognition of the letter at home by talking about their activities and asking them what they learned.

Sincerely,

Your child's teacher

M Is for Mosaic

Materials

roll paper

fat, black marker

colored construction paper

scissors

tacky glue

The Creative Process

- Cut a 2' x 3' sheet from the roll paper. Using a fat, black marker, draw the letter "M" in large block form, filling the entire sheet.
- Set up a cutting center in your room for the children to cut colored construction paper into mosaic pieces to glue onto the large letter "M".
- Hang the letter on the Alphabet Gallery wall.

Personal "M" Mosaics

Materials

tagboard
scissors
glue
colored construction paper

The Creative Process

- Cut pieces of tagboard into the letter "M".
- Encourage the children to cut and tear colored construction paper into small mosaic pieces and glue them onto their own letter "M".

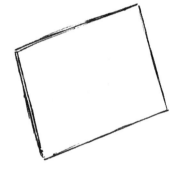

Marble Magic

Materials
tagboard

scissors

tempera paint in a variety of colors

zipper-closure plastic bags

marbles

shoeboxes with lids

The Creative Process
- Cut a piece of tagboard into the shape of a letter "M".
- Squeeze a small amount of tempera paint into a zipper-closure plastic bag. Add a marble to the bag.
- Make several bags using different colors of paint.
- Encourage the children to move each marble around in the bag to cover it completely with paint.
- Place the tagboard letter "M" into the shoebox.
- Drop a few of the paint-covered marbles into the box on top of the letter "M".
- Place the lid onto the box and tip the box in different directions so the marble will roll around.
- Open the lid and take out the marbles and the letter "M".
- Allow it to dry, and then hang it on a bulletin board.

Magnificent Mural

Materials

large roll paper

scissors

masking tape

crayons

The Creative Process

- Cut off a large piece of roll paper and hang it at the children's height on a wall in the hallway or your classroom.
- Brainstorm together some things that begin with the letter "M".
- Ask the children to create a mural by drawing anything that begins with the letter "M".
- Encourage them to give a background to their composition, as well as to fill the paper with their drawings.
- Place a heading above the mural titled: "Our Class' Magnificent Letter "M" Mural."

Our Class' Magnificent Letter "M" Mural

Music Paintings

Materials

cassette tape player or CD player

classical music cassette tape or CD

watercolor paints

paintbrushes

water pans

watercolor paper

The Creative Process

Play classical music and encourage the children to paint with watercolor paints as they listen to the music.

The Bridge Home

Send home the following letter after completing the activities, revising it as necessary.

Dear Parents,

This week, your children learned about the letter "M". Whenever the children see the letter "M" in print and hear it spoken, it reinforces their recognition of the letter. This week, we did a number of art activities with titles that begin with the letter "M" or that develop a concept that begins with the letter "M".

Every week, as an introduction to the new letter, the children do some sort of art activity beginning with that letter on a large outline of the particular letter. This is called the "Alphabet Gallery Activity." I have devoted an entire area in our classroom as the Alphabet Gallery. When the children finish decorating the large letter each week, I add it to the "Gallery" by hanging it on the wall.

This past week, the children made mosaics on a large letter "M" for their Alphabet Gallery activity. The children cut construction paper and glued them onto the large letter. I explained that the word "mosaic" begins with the letter "M". The children also saw the large letter as they made their prints, further reinforcing their recognition of the letter.

The children did various art activities that all began with the letter "M". As an extension of the alphabet gallery activity, the children made mosaics on their own letter "M". They also made designs by putting a tagboard letter "M" into a shoebox, and then dropping paint-covered marbles on top of the "M". They put the lid on and shook the box to create designs. I explained that "marble" begins with the letter "M". They also made murals by drawing anything that begins with the letter "M". We discussed various things that begin with "M" and I also explained what a mural was. Finally, they painted to music.

All of these art activities focused on different things that begin with the letter "M" (mosaic, marble, mural, and music). This reinforced the children's recognition of the letter "M" because we discussed what the words meant, they saw the letter in print, and they heard it spoken. You can help further the children's recognition of the letter at home by talking about their activities and asking them what they learned.

Sincerely,

Your child's teacher

Nuts for the Letter "N"!

Materials

roll paper
fat, black marker
tacky glue
nutshells from a variety of nuts

The Creative Process

- Cut a 2' x 3' sheet from the roll paper. Using a fat, black marker, draw the letter "N" in large block form, filling the entire sheet.
- Encourage the children to glue shells from a variety of nuts on the letter "N".
  Caution: Check for food allergies before doing this activity.
- Hang the letter on the Alphabet Gallery wall.

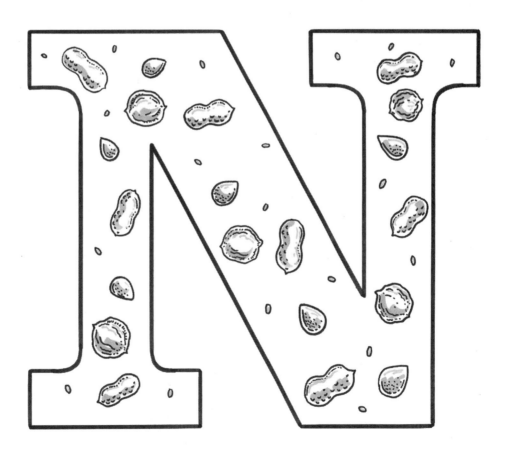

Personal Nutty N's

Materials

tagboard

scissors

glue

shells from a variety of nuts

The Creative Process

- Cut pieces of tagboard into the shape of the letter "N", one for each child.
- Encourage the children to glue nutshells to their letter "N".
- Allow them to dry and hang them on a bulletin board.

Caution: Check for food allergies before doing this activity.

Negative Images

Materials

objects to trace, such as leaves, tools, shoes, child's hand,
    keys, stencils, and so on
white chalk
black construction paper
scissors
white construction paper
glue

The Creative Process

- Help the children trace various objects onto the black
  construction paper using white chalk.
- Next, help them cut along the chalk line and
  glue the paper shapes in an interesting
  composition onto white paper.

More Negative Images

Materials

objects from nature and household items, such as leaves, shells,
    tools, and so on
photo paper

The Creative Process

- Encourage the children to place a variety of objects on a piece of photo paper. Place it in the sun.
- When you remove the objects from the paper, a negative image will be visible.

Art Across the Alphabet

The Bridge Home

Send home the following letter after completing the activities, revising it as necessary.

Dear Parents,

This week, your children learned about the letter "N". Whenever the children see the letter "N" in print and hear it spoken, it reinforces their recognition of the letter. To further reinforce this recognition, we did a number of art activities with titles that begin with the letter "N" or that develop a concept that begins with the letter "N".

Every week, as an introduction to the new letter, the children do some sort of art activity beginning with that letter on a large outline of the particular letter. This is called the "Alphabet Gallery Activity." I have devoted an entire area in our classroom as the Alphabet Gallery. When the children finish decorating the large letter each week, I add it to the "Gallery" by hanging it on the wall.

This past week, the children glued a variety of nutshells on a large letter "N" for their Alphabet Gallery activity. I explained that the word "nut" begins with the letter "N". The children also saw the large letter as they made designs, further reinforcing their recognition of the letter.

The children did various art activities that all began with the letter "N". As an extension of the alphabet gallery activity, the children glued nutshells to their own letter "N". They also learned about "negative images." They made them by tracing objects onto black paper using chalk. Then they cut out the tracings and glued them to white paper. After that, they did another negative image project. They placed a variety of nature and household items on a piece of photo paper and left them in the sun. When they removed the objects, the negative image appeared.

All of these art activities focused on different things that begin with the letter "N" (nutshells and negative image). This reinforced the children's recognition of the letter "N" because we discussed what the words meant, they saw the letter in print, and they heard it spoken. You can help further the children's recognition of the letter at home by talking about their activities and asking them what they learned.

Sincerely,

Your child's teacher

O-Shaped Printing

Materials

roll paper

fat, black marker

orange tempera paint

paint trays

"O"-shaped or circular objects, such as plastic cups in a variety of sizes, soda cans, round blocks, small balls, paper towel tubes, pencil eraser, plastic bracelets, and so on

tacky glue

The Creative Process

- Cut a 2' x 3' sheet from the roll paper. Using a fat, black marker, draw the letter "O" in large block form, filling the entire sheet.
- Pour orange tempera paint into the paint trays.
- Demonstrate how to make prints using the various circular objects by dipping them into the paint and then pressing them onto the letter "O".
- Encourage the children to make prints all over the large letter "O" using various objects.
- Hang the letter on the Alphabet Gallery wall.

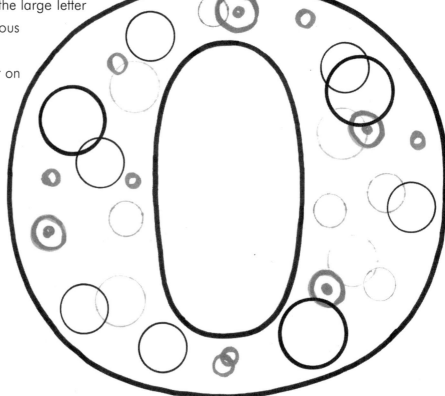

Art Across the Alphabet

Personal Orange O's

Materials

tagboard

scissors

sentence strip

black marker

orange tempera paint

paintbrushes

The Creative Process

- Cut pieces of tagboard into the shape of a letter "O," one for each child.
- Write the word "orange" on a sentence strip using an orange marker. Show it to the children and read the word "orange" out loud.
- Point to the letter "O" and tell the children that the word "orange" begins with the letter "O".
- Encourage the children to paint their tagboard letter "O" with orange paint.
- Allow them to dry, and then hang them on a bulletin board.

Outside Art

Materials

sidewalk chalk
Polaroid camera

The Creative Process

● Take the children outside and encourage them to create a mural on the sidewalk using sidewalk chalk.

● Take photographs of the children as they create.

● Hang the photos on a bulletin board.

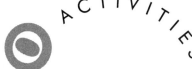

The Bridge Home

Send home the following letter after completing the activities, revising it as necessary.

Dear Parents,

This week, your children learned about the letter "O". Whenever the children see the letter "O" in print and hear it spoken, it reinforces their recognition of the letter. To further reinforce this recognition, we did a number of art activities with titles that begin with the letter "O" or that develop a concept that begins with the letter "O".

Every week, as an introduction to the new letter, the children do some sort of art activity beginning with that letter on a large outline of the particular letter. This is called the "Alphabet Gallery Activity." I have devoted an entire area in our classroom as the Alphabet Gallery. When the children finish decorating the large letter each week, I add it to the "Gallery" by hanging it on the wall.

This past week, the children made prints using orange paint and "O"-shaped objects on a large letter "O" for their Alphabet Gallery activity. I explained that the word "orange" begins with the letter "O". The children also saw the "O" shapes and the large letter as they made designs, further reinforcing their recognition of the letter.

The children did various art activities that all began with the letter "O". As an extension of the alphabet gallery activity, the children made their own orange "O"-shaped prints on their own letter "O". Before they started, I showed them the word "orange" on a sentence strip to reinforce their recognition. They also made "outside art" by drawing a sidewalk mural using chalk. I took photographs of the children's work and posted them on a bulletin board.

All of these art activities focused on different things that begin with the letter "O" (orange and outside). This reinforced the children's recognition of the letter "O" because we discussed what the words meant, they saw the letter in print, and they heard it spoken. You can help further the children's recognition of the letter at home by talking about their activities and asking them what they learned.

Sincerely,

Your child's teacher

P Is for Pig

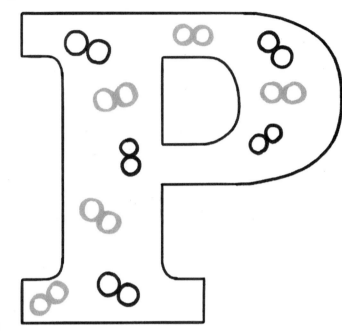

Materials

roll paper

fat, black marker

toilet paper rolls

scissors

hole punch

elastic

sentence strips

pink tempera paint

paint tray

paintbrushes

tacky glue

The Creative Process

- Cut a 2' x 3' sheet from the roll paper. Using a fat, black marker, draw the letter "P" in large block form, filling the entire sheet.
- Make a "pig snout" by cutting an empty toilet paper roll in half and gluing the two halves together, side by side. Make one for each child in the class. Allow to dry.
- Punch a hole into both halves of the toilet paper roll.
- Make a headband for the pig snout by threading a piece of elastic through both holes and tying it in a knot.
- Write the word "pig" on a sentence strip. As you read the word out loud, point to the letter "P" and explain that pig begins with the letter "P".
- Pour pink tempera paint into a paint tray.
- Put on a pig snout and demonstrate how to dip the end of the snout (carefully) into the tray of paint, and then press it onto the letter "P" to make a print.
- Ask each child to repeat this step.
- After everyone has had a turn, ask the children to paint their pig snouts with the pink paint. Allow them to dry before wearing them again.
- Hang the letter on the Alphabet Gallery wall.
- Take a photograph of your "little piggies" wearing their snouts to display on a bulletin board.

Papier-Mâché Puppets

Materials

newspaper

scissors

flour

water

buckets

socks

masking tape

tempera paint

paintbrushes

material scraps

fabric glue

The Creative Process

- Cut or tear newspaper into squares, approximately 2" x 2".
- Mix the water and flour in a bucket, creating a paste similar to pancake batter.
- Ask the children to roll one whole piece of newspaper into a ball.
- Then, demonstrate how to create a "head" by taping the newspaper ball onto a sock with masking tape. Push the toe tip of the sock up into the newspaper head.
- Show the children how to spread a layer of the papier-mâché paste onto the newspaper "head."

Push the toe tip into the ball...

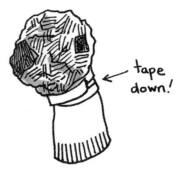

← tape down!

- Place a layer of newspaper squares on the "head," completely covering all the papier-mâché paste. Repeat this process two more times.

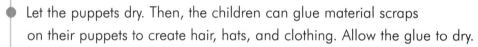

- Allow the puppets to dry.
- Next, encourage the children to paint faces onto their puppets using tempera paint.
- Let the puppets dry. Then, the children can glue material scraps on their puppets to create hair, hats, and clothing. Allow the glue to dry.
- Encourage the children to create a puppet show to perform for another class.

completely cover all the paste...

Amateur Picture-Taking

Materials

disposable camera

The Creative Process

- Using one disposable camera, let the children take turns taking pictures at school and at home.
- Go outside with the children and take a nature walk around the school to provide an opportunity for them to take pictures. Then take a walk through the school to photograph people.

Perfect Pockets

Materials

fabric

scissors

fabric glue

buttons

sequins

rickrack

patches

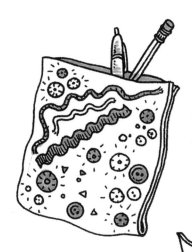

The Creative Process

- Cut fabric into 15" x 18" pieces.
- Help the children fold the fabric pieces in half and glue the front and back of the left and right sides together, leaving the top open. This will create a pocket.
- Encourage the children to decorate their pocket by gluing on various buttons, sequins, rickrack, patches, and so on.

Pretty Paper

Materials

newspaper
bricks
window screens
cookie sheet
scraps of recycled
paper
bender
water
towel
sponges

The Creative Process

- Line a table with newspaper.
- Put the window screen on top of the table. Place one brick underneath each corner of the window screen.
- Slide the cookie sheet underneath the elevated screen.
- Ask the children to tear pieces of scrap paper and place them into the blender.
- Pour a liberal amount of water into the blender, covering the paper scraps. Blend the mixture until the paper and water form a pulp.
- Pour the pulp onto the elevated screen over the section where the cookie sheet is. Spread out the pulp on the screen.
- Place a towel over the pulp and using sponges, press down on the towel where the pulp is squeezing the water out and onto the cookie sheet. Ring out the sponge when it absorbs too much water.
- Repeat the process for each child, using a separate window screen for each child.
- Allow the paper sheets to dry.

The Bridge Home

Send home the following letter after completing the activities, revising it as necessary.

Dear Parents,

This week, your children learned about the letter "P". Whenever the children see the letter "P" in print and hear it spoken, it reinforces their recognition of the letter. To further reinforce this recognition, we did a number of art activities with titles that begin with the letter "P" or that develop a concept that begins with the letter "P".

Every week, as an introduction to the new letter, the children do an art activity beginning with that letter on a large outline of the particular letter. This is called the "Alphabet Gallery Activity." I have devoted an entire area in our classroom as the Alphabet Gallery. When the children finish decorating the large letter each week, I add it to the "Gallery" by hanging it on the wall.

This past week, the children made "pig snout" prints on a large letter "P" for their Alphabet Gallery activity. I made "pig snouts" by gluing two halves of a toilet paper roll together and tying a piece of elastic around them to make a headband. The children put them on and dipped the end of the snout into paint. Then they made prints! I explained that the word "pig" and "print" both begin with the letter "P". The children also saw the large letter as they made designs, further reinforcing their recognition of the letter.

The children did various art activities that all began with the letter "P". They made papier-mâché puppets. I explained what "papier-mâché" was and that it begins with the letter "P". We also went outside and took photographs. The children also made fabric pockets. Finally, the children made "pretty paper." The children tore up paper and put it into a blender. I added water to the paper, and blended it to form a pulp. I spread the pulp on an elevated screen (one for each child) and put a towel over it. Then we used sponges to press down on it. Then we let the paper dry. I explained that "pulp" and "paper" both begin with "P".

All of these art activities focused on different things that begin with the letter "P" (pig, papier-mâché, puppet, pocket, pictures, pulp, and paper). This reinforced the children's recognition of the letter "P" because we discussed what the words meant, they saw the letter in print, and they heard it spoken. You can help further the children's recognition of the letter at home by talking about their activities and asking them what they learned.

Sincerely,

Your child's teacher

Quilted Q

Materials

roll paper

fat, black marker

fabric scraps

scissors

tacky glue

The Creative Process

- Cut a 2' x 3' sheet from the roll paper. Using a fat, black marker, draw the letter "Q" in large block form, filling the entire sheet.
- Cut fabric scraps into small squares.
- Help the children glue the small squares of fabric onto the letter "Q" to create a patchwork quilted letter.
- Hang the letter on the Alphabet Gallery wall.

Art Across the Alphabet

Quality Quilt

Materials

pencils
paper
fabric scraps
scissors
fabric glue
12" x 12" fabric or felt squares
needle and thread or sewing machine
(adult only)

The Creative Process

- Tell the children that you would like them to draw a "self-portrait." Explain that this means to draw a picture of their own face. The pictures do not have to be realistic—even scribbles are fine.

- Next, ask the children to cut various fabric scraps to create their self-portrait in fabric.

- Encourage the children to glue the pieces onto a fabric square.

- Sew all the squares onto a large sheet of fabric to make a quilt. (TIP: Find a parent or caregiver who enjoys sewing to sew the pieces together into the final quilt.)

- Be sure to place the names of the children under their picture as well as the class year on the quilt.

- Hang it in the hallway.

* Author note: If the children in your class can only scribble, it will still look nice. My three-year-old draws faces that only slightly resemble a face, but to him, they look real. However, if you feel that drawing pictures of themselves is too advanced, you can ask the children to just draw any design.

Quill Painting

Materials

drawing paper
fat, black marker
sentence strip
large feather
tempera paint

The Creative Process

- Draw a large, block-style letter "Q" onto a piece of drawing paper, filling the entire page. Make one for each child in the class.
- Write the word "quill" on a sentence strip. Explain to the children that a feather is also called a quill and that it starts with the letter "Q" (point to the letter on the sentence strip).
- Explain that a long time ago, before we had ballpoint pens, people used quills to write.
- Demonstrate how to write with a quill by dipping it into paint and drawing squiggles all over the paper. Then, demonstrate how to dip the feathery end into the paint and paint on the paper to create a different design.
- Ask the children to decorate their own letter "Q" with the quills.
- Allow to dry.

The Bridge Home

Send home the following letter after completing the activities, revising it as necessary.

Dear Parents,

This week, your children learned about the letter "Q". Whenever the children see the letter "Q" in print and hear it spoken, it reinforces their recognition of the letter. This week, we did a number of art activities with titles that begin with the letter "Q" or that develop a concept that begins with the letter "Q".

Every week, as an introduction to the new letter, the children do some sort of art activity beginning with that letter on a large outline of the particular letter. This is called the "Alphabet Gallery Activity." I have devoted an entire area in our classroom as the Alphabet Gallery. When the children finish decorating the large letter each week, I add it to the "Gallery" by hanging it on the wall.

This past week, the children glued small fabric squares onto a large letter "Q" (like a quilt) for their Alphabet Gallery activity. I explained that the word "quilt" begins with the letter "Q". The children also saw the large letter as they made designs, further reinforcing their recognition of the letter.

The children did various art activities that all began with the letter "Q". They drew "self portraits," and then cut fabric into pieces to create their self portrait in fabric. I (or an adult) sewed the squares into a large quilt. The children also learned what the word "quill" means (a feather) and that people used them to write with a long time ago. The children dipped their own quills (feathers) into paint and made designs on their own letter "Q".

All of these art activities focused on different things that begin with the letter "Q" (quilt and quill). This reinforced the children's recognition of the letter "Q" because we discussed what the words meant, they saw the letter in print, and they heard it spoken. You can help further the children's recognition of the letter at home by talking about their activities and asking them what they learned.

Sincerely,

Your child's teacher

Rosy Red

Materials

roll paper

fat, black marker

white, black, and red tempera paint

paintbrushes

Styrofoam egg cartons

tacky glue

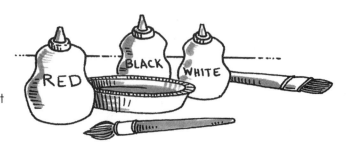

The Creative Process

- Cut a 2' x 3' sheet from the roll paper. Using a fat, black marker, draw the letter "R" in large block form, filling the entire sheet.

- Using Styrofoam egg cartons, help the children mix white tempera paint with red tempera paint to create a lighter red/pink hue, and black tempera paint with red to create a darker red hue.

- Encourage the children to paint the various shades of red onto the large letter "R".

- Hang the letter on the Alphabet Gallery wall.

Rough Sand Painting

Materials

black permanent marker

12" x 12" tagboard squares

tempera paint in a variety of colors

paint pans

sand

paintbrushes

water pans

The Creative Process

- Use a black permanent marker to write the letter "R" on the tagboard squares, touching all edges of the tagboard.
- Pour various colors of tempera paint into paint pans.
- Mix a bit of sand into each pan with the paint.
- Encourage the children to create a Rough Sand Painting on their letter "R".
- They can rinse their brushes between colors using the water pans.

Pet Rock

Materials

large, smooth rocks

scraps of material, sequins, wiggly eyes, buttons, and so on

box

tempera paint

paintbrushes

glue

The Creative Process

- Ask the children to pick a rock to decorate.
- Place the scraps of material, sequins, wiggly eyes, buttons, and other decorating materials into a scrap box.
- Encourage the children create their own "pet rock" by painting their rock and gluing the materials from the scrap box on it.

Rain Painting

Materials

tempera paint in a variety of colors
paintbrushes
large white paper
rainy day

The Creative Process

- On a rainy day, ask the children to paint with tempera paint on large white paper.
- Place the paintings outside in the rain for a few minutes.
- Bring the paintings back inside and discuss the effect the rain had, and the composition it made!

The Bridge Home

Send home the following letter after completing the activities, revising it as necessary.

Dear Parents,

This week, your children learned about the letter "R". Whenever the children see the letter "R" in print and hear it spoken, it reinforces their recognition of the letter. To further reinforce their recognition of the letter "R", we did a number of art activities with titles that begin with the letter "R" or that develop a concept that begins with the letter "R".

Every week, as an introduction to the new letter, the children do some sort of art activity beginning with that letter on a large outline of the particular letter. This is called the "Alphabet Gallery Activity." I have devoted an entire area in our classroom as the Alphabet Gallery. When the children finish decorating the large letter each week, I add it to the "Gallery" by hanging it on the wall.

This past week, the children mixed red paint with black and white paint and painted on a large letter "R" for their Alphabet Gallery activity. They experimented making various shades of red. I explained that the word "red" begins with the letter "R". The children also saw the large letter as they made designs, further reinforcing their recognition of the letter.

The children did various art activities that all began with the letter "R". I added sand to paint to give it a rough finish, and the children used it to make "rough sand" paintings. I explained that "rough" begins with "R". The children decorated rocks to make "pet rocks." Finally, on a rainy day, we made paintings inside and then brought them out into the rain to see what would happen. After we brought them back in, we discussed what the rain did to the paintings.

All of these art activities focused on different things that begin with the letter "R" (red, rough, rock, and rain). This reinforced the children's recognition of the letter "R" because we discussed what the words meant, they saw the letter in print, and they heard it spoken. You can help further the children's recognition of the letter at home by talking about their activities and asking them what they learned.

Sincerely,

Your child's teacher

Stringy S

Materials

roll paper
fat, black marker
thick, colored string
scissors
tacky glue

The Creative Process

- Cut a 2' x 3' sheet from the roll paper. Using a fat, black marker, draw the letter "S" in large block form, filling the entire sheet.
- Cut the string into a variety of lengths.
- Encourage the children to glue strips of thick string onto the letter "S".
- Fill in the entire letter with a variety of colored string.
- Hang the letter on the Alphabet Gallery wall.

Silly Sculpture

Materials

16 GA galvanized steel wire or bendable
  wire hangers
wire cutters (adult only)
4" x 4" wooden blocks or an 8" clay saucer
hot glue gun (adult only)
pantyhose and scissors or knee highs
tape or glue
Gesso (canvas primer)
paintbrushes
tempera paint

The Creative Process

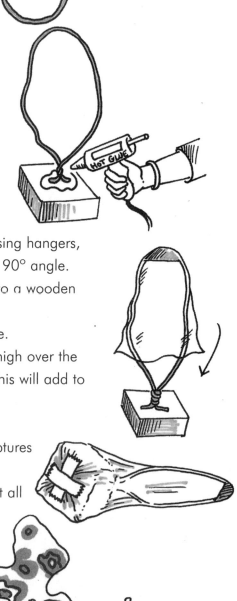

twist the ends...

- Cut the wire into 36" strips (adult only). Cut one strip for each child.
- Bend 1" of both ends and twist them together. If using hangers, bend the end of the hanger used for hanging to a 90° angle.
- Use a hot glue gun (adult only) to attach the wire to a wooden block or clay saucer to make a base.
- If using pantyhose, cut off one leg of the pantyhose.
- Help the children stretch the stocking leg or knee-high over the wire shape and base. If the stocking runs or rips, this will add to the uniqueness of the sculpture.
- Tape or glue the stocking end to the base.
- Encourage the children to bend and form the sculptures to make the desired creation.
- Brush Gesso over the entire form, making sure that all of the stocking is covered completely.
- Once dry, this will become hard.
- After drying, encourage the children to paint their sculptures.
- Display the unique creations!

Art Across the Alphabet

Life-Size Self-Portraits

Materials

tape measure

marker or pen

large roll paper

scissors

crayons

paintbrushes (variety of fat and thin)

tempera paint

tacky glue

newspaper

The Creative Process

- Measure the height of each child, adding 4" to each child's measurement. For example, if a child is 46", mark her height as 50". Then, double each child's measurement (for example, this child is 100").

- Next, measure the child's doubled measurement on the roll paper and cut the piece off.

- Fold each child's paper in half. Ask each child to lie in a creative pose on her roll paper, with the top of her head touching the top folded line. Use a crayon to trace around each child's shape.

- Encourage the children to draw as many details as they can imagine on their self-portraits using a crayon.

- Provide a variety of brush sizes and tempera paint for the children to paint their self- portraits. Allow them to dry.

- Keeping the paper folded in half, cut out the self-portraits. Make sure to cut through the top paper and bottom paper while keeping the folded part at the top of the head uncut. Write the child's name on the portrait.

Don't cut the fold!

leave large space on side unglued

Jacob

- Open the folded self-portrait, and then help the children glue along all the edges of the inside of their paper, leaving a large area on one side unglued. This will allow an open area for stuffing.
- Fold the paper in half again, gluing the sides together. Allow to dry.
- Ask the children to paint the backs of their self-portrait and set them aside to dry.
- Encourage the children to crumple up sheets of newspaper and gently stuff their self-portraits.
- When the stuffing is complete, glue the opening closed.
- Hang the self-portraits together in a hallway for all to enjoy!

Tip

- Encourage some children to pose as if they are doing a handstand and trace around their hair as if they were upside down. Be sure to hang these upside down in the hallway. Encourage the children to create a mural background on which to hang the portraits.

Amelia

Spongy S

Materials

tagboard

fat, black marker

sea sponges

tempera paint

paint trays

The Creative Process

- Draw a large letter "S" onto the tagboard, filling the entire page. Make one for each child.
- Show the children the sea sponges, explaining that they begin with the letter "S".
- Pour paint into paint trays.
- Demonstrate to the children how to dip a sea sponge into the paint and print all over the "S".
- Ask the children to repeat the process to decorate their own letter "S".
- Allow to dry.

The Bridge Home

Send home the following letter after completing the activities, revising it as necessary.

Dear Parents,

This week, your children learned about the letter "S". Whenever the children see the letter "S" in print and hear it spoken, it reinforces their recognition of the letter. To further reinforce this recognition, we did a number of art activities with titles that begin with the letter "S" or that develop a concept that begins with the letter "S".

Every week, as an introduction to the new letter, the children do some sort of art activity beginning with that letter on a large outline of the particular letter. This is called the "Alphabet Gallery Activity." I have devoted an entire area in our classroom as the Alphabet Gallery. When the children finish decorating the large letter each week, I add it to the "Gallery" by hanging it on the wall.

This past week, the children glued a variety of strings onto a large letter "S" for their Alphabet Gallery activity. I explained that the word "string" begins with the letter "S". The children also saw the large letter as they made designs, further reinforcing their recognition of the letter.

The children did various art activities that all began with the letter "S". First they made "silly" sculptures. Then they made life-size self-portraits. Finally, they made prints using sea sponges dipped into paint.

All of these art activities focused on different things that begin with the letter "S" (string, sculpture, self-portrait, and sea sponge). This reinforced the children's recognition of the letter "S" because we discussed what the words meant, they saw the letter in print, and they heard it spoken. You can help further the children's recognition of the letter at home by talking about their activities and asking them what they learned.

Sincerely,

Your child's teacher

Texture Printing

Materials

roll paper
fat, black marker
tempera paint
Styrofoam trays or paper plates
materials with a variety of textures
tacky glue

The Creative Process

- Cut a 2' x 3' sheet from the roll paper. Using a fat, black marker, draw the letter "T" in large block form, filling the entire sheet.
- Pour a small amount of tempera paint into trays or plates.
- Provide materials that have a variety of textures, such as small pieces of carpeting, empty corncobs, blocks of wood, objects from nature, sandpaper, and so on.
- Encourage the children to dip the objects into the paint and make prints on the large letter "T".
- Hang the letter on the Alphabet Gallery wall.

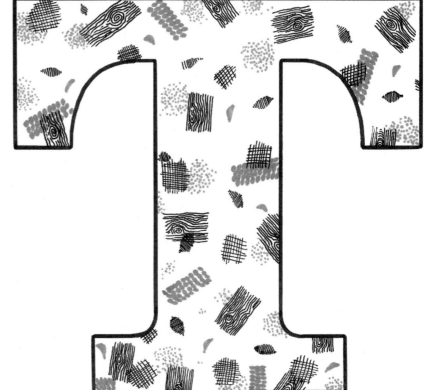

Personal Texture Printing

Materials

12" x 12" pieces of tagboard

black permanent marker

tempera paint

paint trays

objects that have a variety of textures (see Alphabet Gallery Activity)

The Creative Process

● Draw a block letter "T" on tagboard squares, touching each side of the tagboard. Make one for each child.

● Pour a small amount of tempera paint into trays or plates.

● Provide materials that have a variety of textures, such as small pieces of carpeting, empty corncobs, blocks of wood, objects from nature, sandpaper, and so on.

● Encourage the children to dip the objects into the paint and make prints on their letter "T".

Tissue Paper Town Collage

Materials

books and pictures of towns from around the world (see below)
white paper
tissue paper in a variety of colors
white glue
paintbrushes
scissors
black permanent markers

The Creative Process

- Show the children pictures of various towns from around the world. There are many books you can show them about towns, such as *Around Town* by Chris K. Soentpiet, *Mr. Pine's Purple House* by Leonard Kessler, *The Little House* by Virginia Lee Burton, *Towns and Cities* by Patience Coster, *A Town (Walk Around)* by Connie Roop and Peter Geiger Roop, and *Desert Town, Mountain Town, River Town*, and *Prairie Town*, all by Bonnie and Arthur Geisert.
- Discuss with the children some things they might see in a town.
- Give each child a sheet of white paper and a variety of tissue paper.
- Ask the children to use a paintbrush to spread glue all over the white paper.
- Encourage them to cut and tear the tissue paper and press the pieces onto the glue on the white paper.
- Remind them to think about a town as they work. Allow the pictures to dry.
- Next, ask the children to draw a picture of a town on the paper using black permanent markers.
- Encourage the children to fill the page, and add a background to their composition.

Box Town

Materials

books about towns
large cardboard boxes
markers
colored construction paper
glue
camera, optional

The Creative Process

- Throughout the week, read several books to the children about towns and different kinds of homes.
- Create your own town using large cardboard boxes for the children to play in.
- Ask the children to help you make the boxes into different buildings and houses using markers, colored construction paper, and glue.
- If possible, take plenty of photographs!

The Bridge Home

Send home the following letter after completing the activities, revising it as necessary.

Dear Parents,

This week, your children learned about the letter "T". Whenever the children see the letter "T" in print and hear it spoken, it reinforces their recognition of the letter. This week, we did a number of art activities with titles that begin with the letter "T" or that develop a concept that begins with the letter "T".

Every week, as an introduction to the new letter, the children do some sort of art activity beginning with that letter on a large outline of the particular letter. This is called the "Alphabet Gallery Activity." I have devoted an entire area in our classroom as the Alphabet Gallery. When the children finish decorating the large letter each week, I add it to the "Gallery" by hanging it on the wall.

This past week, the children made "texture prints" on a large letter "T" for their Alphabet Gallery activity. The children dipped objects with a variety of textures (such as carpet, sandpaper, objects from nature, and so on) into paint and made prints. I explained that the word "texture" begins with the letter "T". The children also saw the large letter as they made designs, further reinforcing their recognition of the letter.

The children did various art activities that all began with the letter "T". As an extension of the alphabet gallery activity, the children made texture prints on their own letter "T". They also made tissue paper town collages. First I showed them some books about towns and we discussed what kinds of things we could find in a town. Then the children glued tissue paper to white paper to make a town. Finally, they made a box town by decorating a variety of boxes to look like town buildings. I explained before both of these activities that "town" begins with the letter "T".

All of these art activities focused on different things that begin with the letter "T" (texture, tissue paper, and town). This reinforced the children's recognition of the letter "T" because we discussed what the words meant, they saw the letter in print, and they heard it spoken. You can help further the children's recognition of the letter at home by talking about their activities and asking them what they learned.

Sincerely,

Your child's teacher

Unbelievable Umbrellas

Materials

roll paper

fat, black marker

colored construction paper

scissors

markers

glue

tacky glue

The Creative Process

- Cut a 2' x 3' sheet from the roll paper. Using a fat, black marker, draw the letter "U" in large block form, filling the entire sheet.
- Cut out small umbrella shapes from colored construction paper.
- Encourage the children to decorate the little umbrella shapes and glue them onto the large letter "U".
- Hang the letter on the Alphabet Gallery wall.

Art Across the Alphabet

Under-the-Sea Pictures

Materials

pictures of undersea animals
large paper
oil pastels

The Creative Process

● With the children, use a variety of resources, such as books and the Internet, to find pictures of the many exciting animals that live under the sea.

● Give each child a large sheet of paper.

● Encourage the children to create their own underwater picture using oil pastels.

● Ask them to fill the page with their composition.

Underneath and Upside Down Drawings

Materials

drawing paper
masking tape
tables and chairs
crayons

The Creative Process

- Tape pieces of drawing paper underneath the tables and chairs, allowing enough space between each one for the children to lie down.
- Ask the children to lie down on the floor underneath the tables and chairs and look up at their piece of paper and begin drawing. Encourage them to draw whatever pops into their head!

The Bridge Home

Send home the following letter after completing the activities, revising it as necessary.

Dear Parents,

This week, your children learned about the letter "U". Whenever the children see the letter "U" in print and hear it spoken, it reinforces their recognition of the letter. To further reinforce their recognition of the letter "U", we did a number of art activities with titles that begin with the letter "U" or that develop a concept that begins with the letter "U".

Every week, as an introduction to the new letter, the children do some sort of art activity beginning with that letter on a large outline of the particular letter. This is called the "Alphabet Gallery Activity." I have devoted an entire area in our classroom as the Alphabet Gallery. When the children finish decorating the large letter each week, I add it to the "Gallery" by hanging it on the wall.

This past week, the children decorated small construction paper umbrellas and glued them onto a large letter "U" for their Alphabet Gallery activity. I explained that the word "umbrella" begins with the letter "U". The children also saw the large letter as they glued on their umbrellas, further reinforcing their recognition of the letter.

The children did various art activities that all began with the letter "U". They made "under-the-sea" pictures. Together, we found pictures of a variety of animal that live in the sea (using books and the Internet). The children then used oil pastels to make their own painting. Next, the children made "underneath and upside down" drawings. I taped paper underneath chairs and tables, and the children lay underneath them and painted upside down!

All of these art activities focused on different things that begin with the letter "U" (umbrella, underneath, and upside down). This reinforced the children's recognition of the letter "U" because we discussed what the words meant, they saw the letter in print, and they heard it spoken. You can help further the children's recognition of the letter at home by talking about their activities and asking them what they learned.

Sincerely,

Your child's teacher

Violet V

Materials

roll paper

fat, black marker

white and purple tempera paint

paintbrushes

Styrofoam egg cartons

tacky glue

The Creative Process

- Cut a 2' x 3' sheet from the roll paper. Using a fat, black marker, draw the letter "V" in large block form, filling the entire sheet.
- Help the children add white tempera paint to purple to create the color violet.
- Encourage the children to experiment with mixing white and purple in egg cartons to create other shades of violet.
- Ask the children to paint the large letter "V" with the color violet they created.
- Hang the letter on the Alphabet Gallery wall.

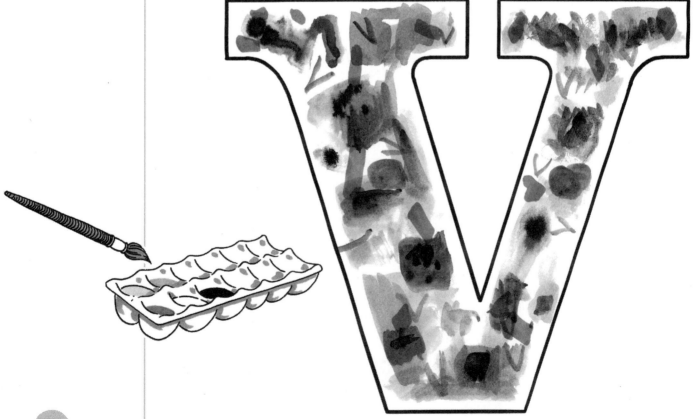

Art Across the Alphabet

Violet V's Painted to Violin Music

Materials

12" x 12" tagboard squares

black permanent marker

scissors

purple tempera paint

white tempera paint

cassette tape player or CD player

cassette tape or CD of violin music

paintbrushes

water pans

The Creative Process

- Draw a letter "V" on the tagboard squares, making sure the letter touches the top and bottom of the tagboard. Make one for each child.
- Cut out the letter "V" for each child.
- Mix white and purple tempera paint to create violet paint.
- While playing violin music, encourage the children to paint their letters with violet paint.
- The children can use the water pans to rinse their brushes between paint colors.

Very Versatile Vase

Materials

self-hardening clay or oven-hardening clay
rolling pin
cup
oven, if needed
tempera paint
paintbrushes

The Creative Process

- Give each child a medium-sized ball of clay. Show the children how to roll the clay flat (about ¼" thick) with a rolling pin.
- Demonstrate how to use a cup to cut out a circle shape from the clay.
- Ask the children to roll the rest of the clay into long, thin, snake-like coils.

- Using the circular-shaped piece of clay as the base, help the children wrap the coils around and on top of the circle and each other to create a vase.
- Encourage them to smooth out the coils when done.
- If the clay needs to be baked, place it into the oven and follow the directions on the package for baking (adult only). If the clay is self-hardening, allow it to dry outside in the sun or by a window.
- Encourage the children to paint their vases with tempera paint.

Velvety Vipers

Materials

velvet or velour material
scissors
tagboard
crayons
tacky glue
tempera paint
small paintbrushes

The Creative Process

- Cut out snake-like shapes in a variety of sizes from velvet or velour material.
- Give each child a piece of tagboard. Ask the children to use crayons to create a picture showing where a snake might want to live.
- Ask the children to glue a velvety viper or two onto their drawing. Allow the glue to dry.
- Encourage the children to paint designs on their viper using tempera paint and small brushes.
- Allow the paint to dry.

The Bridge Home

Send home the following letter after completing the activities, revising it as necessary.

Dear Parents,

This week, your children learned about the letter "V". Whenever the children see the letter "V" in print and hear it spoken, it reinforces their recognition of the letter. This week, we did a number of art activities with titles that begin with the letter "V" or that develop a concept that begins with the letter "V".

Every week, as an introduction to the new letter, the children do some sort of art activity beginning with that letter on a large outline of the particular letter. This is called the "Alphabet Gallery Activity." I have devoted an entire area in our classroom as the Alphabet Gallery. When the children finish decorating the large letter each week, I add it to the "Gallery" by hanging it on the wall.

This past week, the children mixed purple paint with black and white paint and painted on a large letter "V" for their Alphabet Gallery activity. They experimented making various shades of purple. I explained that the word "violet" begins with the letter "V". The children also saw the large letter as they made designs, further reinforcing their recognition of the letter.

The children did various art activities that all began with the letter "V". As an extension of the alphabet gallery activity, the children experimented making shades of violet and painted on their own letter "V". They did this while listening to violin music. I explained that "violet" and "violin" both begin with the letter "V". The children also made their own clay vases. Finally, they made "velvety viper" pictures. I explained that a viper is a snake. I asked them to draw a picture of where a viper might live. Then they cut out viper shapes from velvet or velour material and glued them to their picture.

All of these art activities focused on different things that begin with the letter "V" (violet, violin, vase, velvet, viper). This reinforced the children's recognition of the letter "V" because we discussed what the words meant, they saw the letter in print, and they heard it spoken. You can help further the children's recognition of the letter at home by talking about their activities and asking them what they learned.

Sincerely,

Your child's teacher

Writing Game

Materials

roll paper
fat, black marker
sentence strip
crayons or markers
tacky glue

The Creative Process

- Cut a 2′ x 3′ sheet from the roll paper. Using a fat, black marker, draw the letter "W" in large block form, filling the entire sheet.
- Write the word "writing" on a sentence strip. Show the children the word and tell them what it says. As you point to the letter "W", explain that "writing" begins with that letter.
- Ask the children to write the letter "W" or their name to the best of their ability on the letter "W".
- Hang the letter on the Alphabet Gallery wall. Hang the sentence strip underneath.

Wild Weavings*

This is an easy way for young children to learn how to make a paper weaving, with an extra flair!

*This project requires a bit more teacher-directed instruction until the skill has been accomplished.

Materials

colored construction paper, 8½" x 11" or larger

scissors

ruler

crayons

glue

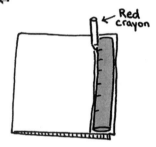

The Creative Process

- Beforehand, cut colored construction paper into 1" strips.
- Ask each child to choose a sheet of colored construction paper. Help the children fold their paper in half.
- Along the edge where the paper meets (not the folded edge), place the ruler flush with the edge and draw a line with a red crayon.
- Help the children draw three, evenly spaced lines with a different colored crayon, starting at the top line down to the folded edge. (For young children, use only two lines.)
- Help the children cut the lines, starting at the folded edge up to (but not through) the red line.
- Help the children write their name on the same side where the red line is.
- On this same side, help the children label the first strip with a letter "X", the second with a letter "O", the third with an "X", and the fourth with an "O" at both the top and bottom.
- Unfold the paper.

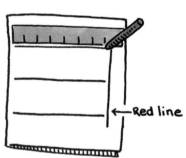

Draw 3 lines with different colors...

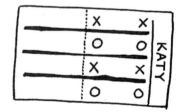

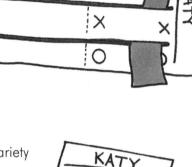

- Ask the children to pick a strip of construction paper and place it under the first "X", over the "O", under the next "X", and so on. When starting the second row, do the opposite of the strip before.

- Encourage the children to weave until no more strips will fit.

- Ask the children to glue down the edges of the strips. Then, they can turn the weaving over and glue down the edges of the strips on that side.

- Encourage the children to be creative and cut out a variety of shapes and sizes from colored construction paper and glue these all over the weaving.

Tips

Don't shy away from using black, white, and brown paper. These colors add great contrast. Try using different types of paper, such as newspaper.

Watercolor Paintings

Materials

paper
watercolor paints
paintbrushes
water pans

The Creative Process

- Give each child a piece of paper.
- Encourage the children to paint a picture using watercolor paints.
- The children can use the water pans to rinse their brushes between paint colors.

"W" Is for White

Materials

white tempera paint
colored construction paper
paintbrushes

The Creative Process

- Encourage the children to paint with white tempera paint on colored construction paper.
- Provide a variety of brush sizes for a different effect.

The Bridge Home

Send home the following letter after completing the activities, revising it as necessary.

Dear Parents,

This week, your children learned about the letter "W". Whenever the children see the letter "W" in print and hear it spoken, it reinforces their recognition of the letter. To further reinforce their recognition of the letter "W", we did a number of art activities with titles that begin with the letter "W" or that develop a concept that begins with the letter "W".

Every week, as an introduction to the new letter, the children do some sort of art activity beginning with that letter on a large outline of the particular letter. This is called the "Alphabet Gallery Activity." I have devoted an entire area in our classroom as the Alphabet Gallery. When the children finish decorating the large letter each week, I add it to the "Gallery" by hanging it on the wall.

This past week, the children wrote the letter "W" or their own name on a large letter "W" for their Alphabet Gallery activity. Beforehand, I showed them the word "writing" on a sentence strip, and we discussed what the word meant. I explained that the word "writing" begins with the letter "W". The children also saw the large letter as they wrote on it, further reinforcing their recognition of the letter.

The children did various art activities that all began with the letter "W". They made construction paper weavings. They painted with watercolor paints, and they painted with white tempera paint on colored construction paper.

All of these art activities focused on different things that begin with the letter "W" (weaving, watercolor, and white). This reinforced the children's recognition of the letter "W" because we discussed what the words meant, they saw the letter in print, and they heard it spoken. You can help further the children's recognition of the letter at home by talking about their activities and asking them what they learned.

Sincerely,

Your child's teacher

eXotic Butterflies

Materials

roll paper

fat, black marker

paper

scissors

pictures of exotic butterflies

markers

tacky glue

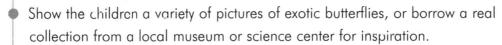

The Creative Process

- Cut a 2' x 3' sheet from the roll paper. Using a fat, black marker, draw the letter "X" in large block form, filling the entire sheet.
- Cut paper into 2" x 2" squares.
- Show the children a variety of pictures of exotic butterflies, or borrow a real collection from a local museum or science center for inspiration.
- Ask each child to draw an exotic butterfly on the pieces of paper using brightly colored markers.
- Write each child's name on his butterfly.
- Ask the children to glue their butterflies onto the large letter "X".
- Hang the letter on the Alphabet Gallery wall.

Personal eXotic Butterflies

Materials

muslin material
scissors
newspaper
fabric paint
paintbrushes
safety pins
yarn

The Creative Process

- Cut 2' wide, fat, oval shapes from the muslin. Cut two for each child. These will be the butterfly wings.
- Cover a table with newspaper and place the wing cutouts on top of the newspaper.
- Encourage the children to decorate their wings using the fabric paint.
- Allow the wings to dry.
- Using two safety pins per child, carefully pin one wing onto the child's shirt at his right shoulder and one onto the child's shirt at his left shoulder.
- Loosely tie a piece of yarn around the child's wrist with the wing pulled through it to hold it in place.
- Encourage the children to fly around the room and outside. They can pretend to fly from flower to flower, or they can make cocoons around themselves and emerge as a beautiful butterfly.

X-ray eXamination!

Materials

variety of fruits and vegetables

cutting knife (adult only)

books and posters of Georgia O'Keefe's artwork

large paper

pencils

crayons

watercolor paints

thin paintbrushes

water pans

The Creative Process

- Prepare the fruits and vegetables by cutting them in half (adult only). Place them on the tables.
- Show the Georgia O'Keefe prints to the children. Explain that the artist always filled the page with her picture as if she were looking through a magnifying glass at the object.
- Ask each child to choose one of the fruits or vegetables on the table to draw.
- Give each child a large sheet of paper. Encourage them to use pencils to draw what they see on the inside of the fruit or vegetable, as if they were using "x-ray" vision.
- Ask them to make their drawing touch all four edges of their paper, and to notice and draw the details.
- Next, ask the children to trace over their pencil lines with crayons, pressing hard.
- Encourage the children to paint in the white areas of their picture with watercolor paints.
- They can use the water pans to rinse their brushes between colors.
- Dry and display.

Art Across the Alphabet

eXtreme X Sculpture

Materials

paper towel or wrapping paper rolls
tacky glue
tempera paint
paintbrushes

The Creative Process

- Give each child two empty paper towel or wrapping paper rolls.
- Help the children glue their two tubes together to create an "X". Allow the glue to dry.
- Encourage the children to decorate their letter "X" sculpture using tempera paint. Allow the paint to dry.

The Bridge Home

Send home the following letter after completing the activities, revising it as necessary.

Dear Parents,

This week, your children learned about the letter "X". Whenever the children see the letter "X" in print and hear it spoken, it reinforces their recognition of the letter. This week, we did a number of art activities with titles that begin with the letter "X" or that develop a concept that begins with the letter "X".

Every week, as an introduction to the new letter, the children do some sort of art activity beginning with that letter on a large outline of the particular letter. This is called the "Alphabet Gallery Activity." I have devoted an entire area in our classroom as the Alphabet Gallery. When the children finish decorating the large letter each week, I add it to the "Gallery" by hanging it on the wall.

This past week, the children glued "eXotic butterflies" on a large letter "X" for their Alphabet Gallery activity. I showed the children pictures of exotic butterflies. Then each child drew his own "exotic" butterfly and glued it to the letter. I explained that the word "exotic" doesn't begin with the letter "X", but has the letter "X" in it. The children also saw the large letter as they made designs, further reinforcing their recognition of the letter.

The children did various art activities that all began with the letter "X". As an extension of the alphabet gallery activity, the children made their own "exotic" butterfly wings. I gave each child two large oval shapes (cut from muslin) to decorate. After the wings were dry, I pinned the children's wings to their shoulders. I then loosely tied a piece of yarn around each child's wrist, attached to the wings, so they could "fly." The children also learned about x-rays. I showed them paintings by the artist, Georgia O'Keefe. I then showed the children various fruits and vegetables cut in half. I encouraged them to draw the insides of these fruits and vegetables (like an "x-ray"). Finally, the children made "extreme X sculptures" by decorating paper towel tubes glued into an "X" shape.

All of these art activities focused on different things that have the letter "X" in their title (exotic, x-ray, examination, and extreme). This reinforced the children's recognition of the letter "X" because we discussed what the words meant, they saw the letter in print, and they heard it spoken. You can help further the children's recognition of the letter at home by talking about their activities and asking them what they learned.

Sincerely,

Your child's teacher

Yards of Yarn

Materials

roll paper

fat, black marker

pencils

white glue

yarn in a variety of colors

tacky glue

The Creative Process

- Cut a 2' x 3' sheet from the roll paper. Using a fat, black marker, draw the letter "Y" in large block form, filling the entire sheet.
- Ask each child to draw a simple design on one part of the large letter "Y".
- Then, encourage them to place glue on top of their design and then wind yarn around it to fill it in.
- Hang the letter on the Alphabet Gallery wall.

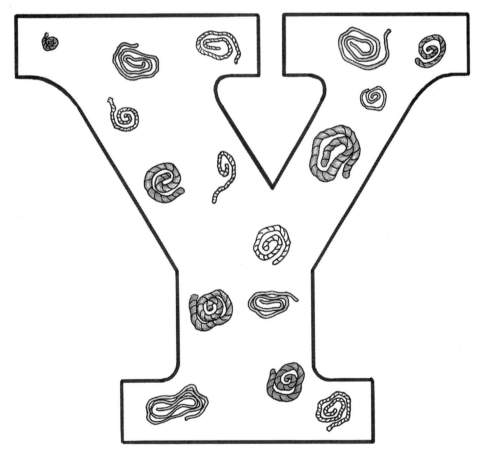

Personal Yards of Yarn

Materials

tagboard squares
pencils
white glue
yarn in a variety of colors

The Creative Process

- Give each child a tagboard square. Ask them to fill the tagboard by drawing large, simple designs without too many small details.
- Help the children place glue on a section of the design and wind yarn around it to fill in the picture and add color.
- Help the children fill in their pictures with the glue and yarn.
- Allow the designs to dry, and then hang them around the room or in the hallway.

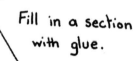

Fill in a section with glue.

Modern Art!

Coil yarn over the shapes.

Yachts of Fun

Materials

thick cardboard

scissors

Popsicle sticks

tacky glue

tempera paint and paintbrushes or markers

The Creative Process

- Cut the thick cardboard into 12" x 12" squares. Give one to each child.
- Explain to the children that a yacht is actually a large boat. (Emphasize that it begins with the letter "Y".)
- Encourage the children to create their own yachts using Popsicle sticks. Demonstrate how to use the cardboard square as a base upon which to build.
- Allow the glue to dry.
- Ask the children to decorate their "yachts" using markers or tempera paint.
- Allow the paint to dry.

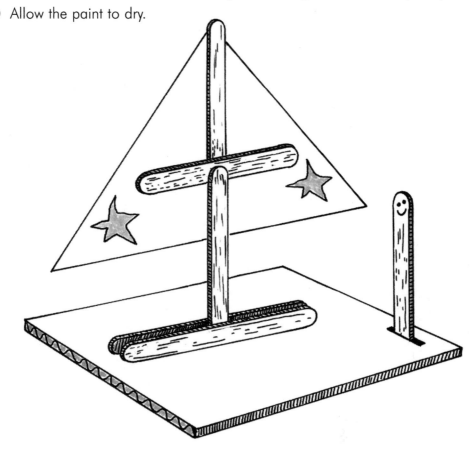

The Bridge Home

Send home the following letter after completing the activities, revising it as necessary.

Dear Parents,

This week, your children learned about the letter "Y". Whenever the children see the letter "Y" in print and hear it spoken, it reinforces their recognition of the letter. To further reinforce this recognition, we did a number of art activities with titles that begin with the letter "Y" or that develop a concept that begins with the letter "Y".

Every week, as an introduction to the new letter, the children do some sort of art activity beginning with that letter on a large outline of the particular letter. This is called the "Alphabet Gallery Activity." I have devoted an entire area in our classroom as the Alphabet Gallery. When the children finish decorating the large letter each week, I add it to the "Gallery" by hanging it on the wall.

This past week, the children made yarn designs on a large letter "Y" for their Alphabet Gallery activity. Each child drew a design on part of the large letter. Then they glued yarn on top of their design. I explained that the word "yarn" begins with the letter "Y". The children also saw the large letter as they made designs, further reinforcing their recognition of the letter.

The children did various art activities that all began with the letter "Y". As an extension of the alphabet gallery activity, the children made yarn designs on their own letter "Y". They also made their own Popsicle yachts. I explained that a "yacht" is a large boat and that it begins with the letter "Y". The children glued the Popsicle sticks to thick cardboard squares and decorated them with paint.

All of these art activities focused on different things that have the letter "Y" in their title (yarn and yacht). This reinforced the children's recognition of the letter "Y" because we discussed what the words meant, they saw the letter in print, and they heard it spoken. You can help further the children's recognition of the letter at home by talking about their activities and asking them what they learned.

Sincerely,

Your child's teacher

Zany Zoo Animal Z

Materials

roll paper

fat, black marker

zoo animal stamps or sponges and scissors

tempera paint and paper plates or ink pads

tacky glue

The Creative Process

- Cut a 2' x 3' sheet from the roll paper. Using a fat, black marker, draw the letter "Z" in large block form, filling the entire sheet.
- Cut sponges into zoo animal shapes, or use zoo animal stamps.
- Encourage the children to dip the sponges into tempera paint, or use the stamps and ink pads to make zoo animal prints all over the large letter "Z".
- Hang the letter on the Alphabet Gallery wall.

Zippy Z's

Materials

roll paper
fat, black marker
tacky glue
zippers

The Creative Process

- Cut a 2' x 3' sheet from the roll paper. Using a fat, black marker, draw the letter "Z" in large block form, filling the entire sheet.
- Encourage the children to glue zippers to the large letter "Z".

Personal Zany Zoo Animal Z's

Materials

12" x 12" tagboard squares

black marker

scissors

zoo animal stamps or sponges and scissors

tempera paint and paper plates or ink pads

The Creative Process

- Draw a letter "Z" on the tagboard, filling the page. Make one for each child.
- Cut out the letters and give one to each child.
- Cut sponges into zoo animal shapes, or use zoo animal stamps.
- Encourage the children to dip the sponges into tempera paint, or use the stamps and ink pads to make zoo animal prints on the individual letter "Z".

Personal Zippy Z's

Materials

12" x 12" tagboard squares

scissors

zippers

white glue

The Creative Process

- Draw a letter "Z" on the tagboard, filling the page. Make one for each child.
- Cut out the letters and give one to each child.
- Ask the children to glue zippers onto the letter "Z" to take home.

Zoo Animal Crayon Resist

Materials

pictures of zoo animals
magnifying glasses
paper
crayons
watercolor paint
paintbrushes

The Creative Process

- Show the children pictures of zoo animals. If possible, visit the zoo, too!
- Discuss the different markings on the various animals.
- Using photographs and picture books, show the children how to look through a magnifying glass to enlarge a section of the animal.
- Demonstrate how to draw an enlarged section of the animal that fills the page.
- Ask each child to pick an animal photo to use to draw. Then, encourage them to use a magnifying glass to draw one section of the animal.
- Next, ask them to go over all the lines with crayons, pressing hard. If desired, the children can fill in a section or two with the crayon; however, explain that they should leave some spots empty to fill in with watercolor paints.
- Encourage the children to use the watercolor paints to fill in the rest of the design. Allow them to dry.
- Create a bulletin board with the pictures and invite the children to guess each animal.

The Bridge Home

Send home the following letter after completing the activities, revising it as necessary.

Dear Parents,

This week, your children learned about the letter "Z". Whenever the children see the letter "Z" in print and hear it spoken, it reinforces their recognition of the letter. To further reinforce their recognition of the letter "Z", we did a number of art activities with titles that begin with the letter "Z" or that develop a concept that begins with the letter "Z".

Every week, as an introduction to the new letter, the children do some sort of art activity beginning with that letter on a large outline of the particular letter. This is called the "Alphabet Gallery Activity." I have devoted an entire area in our classroom as the Alphabet Gallery. When the children finish decorating the large letter each week, I add it to the "Gallery" by hanging it on the wall.

This past week, the children made zoo animal prints on a large letter "Z" for their Alphabet Gallery activity. I pre-cut sponges into a variety of zoo animal shapes and the children pressed the sponges into paint and onto the "Z" to make prints. I explained that the word "zoo" begins with the letter "Z". The children also saw the large letter as they made designs, further reinforcing their recognition of the letter.

The children did various art activities that all began with the letter "Z". As an extension of the alphabet gallery activity, the children made zoo animal prints on their own letter "Z". They also made a "zoo animal crayon resist." The children looked at pictures of a variety of animals with a magnifying glass and we discussed the various markings on the animals. I demonstrated how to draw an enlarged section of the animal to fill an entire page. Then the children drew their own designs with crayons. Finally, they painted over their crayon design with watercolor paints (this is a "resist"). The children also glued zippers onto their own letter "Z".

All of these art activities focused on different things that have the letter "Z" in their title (zoo animal and zipper). This reinforced the children's recognition of the letter "Z" because we discussed what the words meant, they saw the letter in print, and they heard it spoken. You can help further the children's recognition of the letter at home by talking about their activities and asking them what they learned.

Sincerely,

Your child's teacher

Note to teacher: If you decide to do the alternate activity "Zippy Z's", change letter accordingly.

Art Across the Alphabet

Index

Creating Readers
Over 1000 Games, Activities, Tongue Twisters,
Fingerplays, Songs, and Stories to Get Children Excited
About Reading
Pam Schiller

**Simple games and activities to help children learn the
sound of every letter in the alphabet.**

Learn the basic building blocks of reading with *Creating
Readers*, the comprehensive resource that develops a strong
foundation for pre-readers. *Creating Readers* gives teachers
and parents the tools to teach pre-reading skills with over
1000 activities, games, fingerplays, songs, tongue twisters,
poems, and stories for the letters of the alphabet. This
invaluable resource develops the child's desire to read as
well as the skills needed to begin reading. *Creating
Readers* starts children ages 3 to 8 towards a future rich
with books and reading. 448 pages. 2001.

ISBN 978-087659-258-8 / Gryphon House 16375

Preschool Art
It's the Process, Not the Product
MaryAnn F. Kohl

Over 200 activities encourage
children to explore and understand
their world through art experiences
that emphasize the process of art, not the product.
The first chapter introduces basic art activities appropriate
for all children, while the subsequent chapters, which build
on the basic activities in the first chapter, are divided by sea-
sons. Activities are included for painting, drawing, collage,
sculpture, and construction. Indexes organized by art medi-
um and project name help teachers plan. 260 pages.
1994.

ISBN 978-0-87659-168-0 / Gryphon House / 16985

Available
at your favorite
bookstore, school supply
store, or order from
Gryphon House at
800.638.0928 or
www.gryphonhouse.com.